STAR WARS®
DARK FORCES™

Soldier For The Empire

STAR WARS®
DARK FORCES™

Soldier For The Empire

Written by
WILLIAM C. DIETZ

Illustrated by
DEAN WILLIAMS

First Published in Great Britain by
Boxtree Limited
Broadwall House
21 Broadwall
London SE1 9PL

Editors
LYNN ADAIR
GINJER BUCHANAN
& ALLAN KAUSCH

Jacket and book designers
JULIE GASSAWAY
& BRIAN GOGOLIN

Book design manager
BRIAN GOGOLIN

Soldier for the Empire calligrapher
ARTHUR BAKER

This trilogy of graphic story albums is based on the characters and
situations from LucasArts' DARK FORCES and JEDI KNIGHT games and
would not have been possible without the invaluable assistance of Justin
Chin and the development staff of LucasArts Entertainment Company.

This is book one of a trilogy of titles:
Star Wars®: Dark Forces™ — Soldier for the Empire,
Rebel Agent, and *Jedi Knight*.

A CIP catalogue entry for this book
is available from the British Library.

ISBN: 0-7522-2415-8

Printed in Canada

1 3 5 7 9 10 8 6 4 2

*To Ron and Roberta
Ward — who agreed to serve
if called upon — and deserve
nothing but the best.*

*My thanks to Dean Williams
for the art that graces this
book, to Justin Chin and the
development staff of LucasArts
Entertainment Company that
created DARK FORCES, to
the eternally helpful Lucy
Autrey Wilson, Allan Kausch,
David Scroggy, Lynn Adair, Ginjer
Buchanan, and last, but certainly
not least, George Lucas and the other
minds who created this universe.
May the Force be with you.*

BILL DIETZ

*To God, my mother and father,
and to my best friend and fiancée,
Debra. And to Meridian.*

DEAN WILLIAMS

Soldier For The Empire

CHAPTER 1

The relay that failed, and thereby saved Morgan Katarn's life, was an integral part of the pumping station that served the southeast quadrant of his homestead. Without the relay and the pump, his variform beans would wither and die. They, like the rest of the crops, needed the water that Morgan's one-thousand-year-old tap tree brought to the surface via tubular roots, or "taps" that descended hundreds of feet to siphon water from the underlying aquifer — water that was shared with Morgan's crops via endless lengths of imported irrigation tubing.

The workshop was a spacious area in which Morgan spent nearly all his time, when he was home, that is — which was less than he would have liked. His responsibilities as an agro-mech craftsman took more hours away than was good for the farming he did on the side — as did the resistance movement. In the workshop were cupboards where his spare parts were stored, countertops strewn with tools, and bins filled with printouts, schematics, and designs. Morgan circled the worktable to peer at one of six monitors. It provided a rotating 3-D view of the pump's inner workings. The lines that described the offending relay had changed from green to red and blinked on and off. Annoying — but easy to remedy.

Morgan made a note of the part number, opened a storage cabinet, found the matching box, and removed it. A puff of air touched the back of his neck and he heard Wee Gee's cooling fans. He turned and grinned. "Hey, old boy . . . how's that solar panel? All fixed? Good work."

Morgan had designed the droid himself. Since he was a self-taught roboticist, it hadn't been easy. Form had been allowed to follow function

— and Wee Gee looked anything but human. Though capable of assuming hundreds of configurations, Wee Gee always reverted to an inverted U shape. His right arm was three times more powerful than his left. It boasted no less than four articulated joints, and a C-shaped grasper. The left arm was less sturdy but was mounted with a human-style hand that could use the tools carried on the utility belt cinched around Wee Gee's processor housing.

What Morgan called the drive assembly linked both sides of the droid together — and served as a platform for the vertical sensor pod that provided Wee Gee with the electronic equivalent of sight. Thanks to a repulsorlift engine salvaged from an Imperial speeder bike, and steering jets adapted from a junked probe droid, the machine floated two meters off the ground. An oval-shaped lens tilted toward Morgan and the droid made a chirruping sound. The human nodded in response.

"Sure, we'll tackle that in the morning. First things first, though . . . I've got to replace a part on pump four. You're in charge till I get back."

Wee Gee squeaked agreeably and plugged himself into one of the many data ports scattered around the complex. Once connected, the droid could monitor the entire farm from that single position.

The farmer considered a vehicle and decided against it. The walk would be good for both his spirits and his waistline. Morgan checked to ensure that his comlink was charged, grabbed the walking stick from a corner, and slipped through the door.

He took a breath of the crisp evening air and paused to watch Sullust rise. Morgan had friends there, many of whom belonged to the Alliance and were working towards the day when the New Order would be destroyed. That was no small task on a planet where the Emperor ruled through the vast SoroSuub Corporation. Still, where there's a will there's a way, and they would succeed, Morgan was certain.

Walking briskly so as to raise his heart rate to aerobic levels, the farmer struck out towards the southeast. Dry grass crackled beneath his boots, lume bugs danced before his face, and stars appeared in the sky. They reminded Morgan of his son Kyle — and the fact that he would graduate soon.

The thought that financial necessity rather than free choice had played a major role in Kyle's decision to attend the Imperial Military Academy still filled Morgan with guilt. The Katarns were from the Outer Rim, with limited financial resources, and the Academy had represented Kyle's best chance for a good education.

Morgan frowned. Perhaps if he'd been a little more flexible, a little

less focused on *how* money was made, there would be more of it. What would Kyle be like when he returned? Like the boy he'd said good-bye to? Or like the stormtroopers who swaggered through the spaceport? The stars were silent, the lume bugs danced, and there was no way to know.

───── ≍✦≍ ─────

The *Vengeance* was not one of the Empire's larger Star Destroyers, nor was such a vessel required for the matter at hand. After all, why use a sword when a dagger would suffice? The thought pleased the mind that conceived it. The bridge was large and open. The crew stood in semi-circular trenches cut into the highly polished deck. The Dark Jedi known as Jerec stood above the command pit and stared at the moon that floated beyond.

What *he* saw was a great deal more complex than what those around him perceived. Jerec was tall and thin to the point of emaciation. He kept his head shaved and black facial tattoos glowed on his brown skin. Empty eye sockets were hidden behind a band of black leather. His tunic, trousers, and boots were black. Jerec wore no insignia other than the symbols visible on his blood-red collar — and kept his Jedi abilities secret.

Such was the nature of the man, however, and the power he commanded, that no signs of authority were necessary. Jerec acted under orders from Emperor Palpatine himself and looked forward to the day when *all* would kneel before him, though he was careful to hide such ambitions behind a veneer of loyalty.

Captain Thrawn stood behind Jerec, slightly to his right. He was as tall as Jerec but the similarity ended there. Thrawn had shimmering blue-black hair, pale blue skin, and glowing red eyes, all of which testified to his alien origins and were rare in the Empire's xenophobic navy. However, much as Palpatine might distrust other sentient species, he loved a winner, and Thrawn had collected more victories, medals, and promotions than most officers with twice his years of service. He stood with hands clasped behind his back and waited for his superior to speak. When the words came, Jerec's voice was soft, almost feminine. "The probe returned?"

"Yes, sir. There was no sign of a security breach. Surprise will be complete."

"The drop ship is ready?"

"Yes, sir. Loaded and ready."

"Excellent. You may begin."

"Yes, sir."

Thrawn had turned, and was about to leave, when Jerec spoke again. "One more thing . . . "

The officer turned at the sound of Jerec's voice. "Sir?"

"I want Morgan Katarn alive."

Thrawn was well aware of what Jerec wanted but nodded dutifully and said, "Yes, sir," with exactly the same intonation he had used the first time the order had been issued. Besides being a brilliant tactician, and even better strategist, Thrawn had still another virtue, and that was his absolute lack of ego. Something of a necessity for an officer with alien origins in a military organization rife with patronage and politics.

Jerec, who wanted a great deal more than the next pathetic rank in another being's power structure, nodded and stalked away.

Thus dismissed, Thrawn tackled the business at hand. Orders had been given and he would carry them out.

⊶⊷ ⊨⊹⊨ ⊶⊷

Though roughly the same size as an Imperial assault shuttle, the Corellian-built stock light freighter had less armament and still bore the scars accumulated while running supplies to Space Station Kwenn. Captured with a hold full of black-market technics, she'd been added to the rag-tag collection of ships the Empire used for clandestine missions. She was typical of vessels pressed into service by the Alliance. Painted with registration numbers identical to those worn by one of their commerce raiders, she made a believable stand-in for the real thing. Retros fired as she matched velocities with Sulon and prepared to land.

Within her hull, in a cargo compartment that still stank of the hydroponic supplies she had carried, a team of Special Operations commandos prepared for combat. Their leader, a thirty-something first lieutenant named Brazack, watched with all-seeing eyes. He had earned his commission the hard way — in a battle so bloody, every single one of his superiors had been killed. His subsequent promotion came in the wake of a mission that produced no less than four medals of valor — all awarded posthumously.

His peers, almost all of whom had graduated from the Academy, resented Brazack and his almost mystical linkage with the troops assigned to him. In this case, his troops were the second platoon, B company, of the legendary Special Ops Group, also known as the Ghost Battalion.

In spite of their common membership in one of the Empire's most elite military organizations, every single member of the platoon was dressed in a rag-tag collection of mismatched clothes and armor meant to resemble what volunteer elements of the Alliance wore.

And the disguises would have been believable if it weren't for the standard-issue weapons they carried — and the fact that they were exclusively human, a rare circumstance where Reb units were concerned.

Brazack had objected to these discrepancies, and argued for a delay while they were remedied, but was overruled. He reacted the way he always did, with a shrug and a lopsided grin. And why not? It made no difference to Brazack if someone saw through the fiction, especially in light of the fact that he had lodged his protest in writing and retained a computer-generated receipt. Such precautions were second nature to someone who'd risen from the ranks.

The pilot announced, "Three to dirt," and Brazack walked slowly down the center corridor. He made eye contact with each member of the team as he spoke. "All right, men, you know the drill. We land, secure the Landing Zone, and collect the prisoner. Questions? No? Good! Nail this sucker and the drinks are on me."

The men grinned. They knew most officers would hardly acknowledge their status as human beings — much less buy them drinks. Which had everything to do with the fact that they would rather die than disappoint their leader.

The freighter came in out of the sun, sank to rooftop level, and opened up on the farm south of Morgan Katarn's. It belonged, they had been told, to a family named Danga. Lasers burped, buildings burst into flames, and variform cattle broke free of their holding pens. The Imperial pilot, a Caridian named Vester, grinned and circled for another pass. Give the groundies plenty of time for an ID, that's what the briefing said, and that's what he'd do.

A woman and two children broke from the cover provided by the fiercely burning farmhouse and ran for a nearby gully. Vester kicked the ship to the left, centered their images in the heads-up sight, and pressed a button. There was a satisfying flash as the colonists died.

"Missile . . . " his co-pilot said matter-of-factly, well aware of the fact that the freighter was way too low for the shoulder-launched device to arm itself, and fired a waist turret in reply. Bolts of energy hit the center of the vehicle park, marched towards the maintenance shed, and found Don Danga trying to reload. The shoulder-launched missile exploded and he disappeared.

The freighter shuddered, steadied, and headed north. By attacking the Danga farm prior to hitting the Katarn place, and greasing still another family on the way out, they hoped to create the impression of a hit-and-run Rebel raid. Vester didn't much care so long as he did all of the shooting and someone else did all of the dying. He chinned the intercom button. "Okay, Lieutenant . . . thirty to dirt."

Brazack acknowledged the message, took one last look at his men, and stood on the belly ramp. He took pride in leading from the front — and planned to be the first one out.

Vester watched the Katarn farm grow larger, swerved to avoid an enormous tree, and lit his repulsors. The ship staggered, caught itself, and pancaked in. Not very pretty — but ideal when seconds count.

Brazack felt the skids hit, slapped the button next to the hatch, and dived through the opening. He executed a shoulder roll, allowed forward momentum to bring him up, and opened fire. That would keep down the heads of anyone waiting in the farmhouse. Windows shattered and curtains started to smolder. No one fired in return. The platoon poured out of the ship, formed a skirmish line, and waited for orders.

Vester waited till the commandos were clear, lit his repulsors, and departed northward. His job was to inflict additional damage, provide fire support if called upon to do so, and make the final pickup. A quick check confirmed that a flight of five TIE fighters had secured his escape route. The mission was on the rails and Vester was happy.

⋯⋯ ⊱◊⊰ ⋯⋯

Morgan Katarn had arrived on the south slope of the hill that stood between his house and the southeast quad when he heard the rumble of in-system engines and saw the low-flying ship. He viewed the vessel as little more than a curiosity at first, a pilot so stupid that he or she had missed the spaceport to the east and was searching for landmarks. Then he noticed that the running lights had been extinguished and that the vessel was flying below official minimums, and his stomach felt funny. That kind of feeling had protected him in the past.

Within a fraction of a second from the time the doubts first entered his mind, the ship opened fire. Morgan stood stunned as lasers stabbed the ground, an SLM went off high above, and something exploded.

Morgan fumbled the electrobinoculars out of their belt pouch and brought them up to his eyes. The device captured what light there was, enhanced it, and fed the results to the eyepiece. By pressing "zoom" followed by "record" Morgan was able to document what was happening.

⇥◆⇤

The Katarn house was a modest structure, only half of which appeared aboveground. The rest, for reasons of cost and insulation, was surrounded by carefully packed earth.

Brazack waited for Corporal Koyo to kick the door in, waited for defensive fire that never came, and entered with his weapon at ready. The living room had a dusty, unlived-in feel, as if it was more for show than use, and contained little of value or interest. Brazack pointed toward a pair of doors. "Koyo . . . Santo . . . see where those go. And keep your eyes peeled for Katarn."

The men had memorized Morgan's face during the simulation briefing. They managed to withhold the "Yes, sirs" that came naturally to their lips and said "Gotcha," instead.

Rank hath privilege and Brazack had assigned the most interesting avenue of investigation to himself. It led through an archway and into a workshop. He had no more than passed through the entryway when something struck him in the chest and threw him backward. The armor beneath his shirt prevented serious injury but it hurt nonetheless. The missile consisted of a partially disassembled servo mechanism, and in spite of the fact that Wee Gee had thrown the device with unerring accuracy, the threat index was extremely low. However, the commandos reacted as they would to any threat, and used overwhelming force.

The antipersonnel grenade hit the floor, launched itself into the air, and exploded. The droid squeaked pitifully. Santo put a beam through the machine's speaker grill. Wee Gee considered further resistance, decided against it, and sent an electronic warning to Morgan Katarn.

⇥◆⇤

High on the hill behind the farm Morgan both heard and felt his beeper go off, knew the raiders had found Wee Gee, and touched the button that would silence it. A lump formed in his throat. Yes, Wee Gee was a machine, but he'd been a friend as well.

Helpless to do anything more than document what transpired, the farmer saw fires appear among his outbuildings, and saw the ship return from the north and squat in front of his house. There was something about the raiders that bothered Morgan. It eluded him at first, but then he had it. The so-called Rebels carried identical weapons! Not to mention that every single one of them was human. They *looked* like Rebels, but they *weren't* Rebels, so what did that leave? The simple answer, the obvious answer, was Imperial troops. Sent to kill and/or capture Reb leaders. That would explain the attack.

Morgan dropped to the ground as the ship fired repulsors and rose into the air. Fires, the last ones no larger than sparks, marked the ship's passage to the west. Morgan shook his head sadly. If the Imperials thought such raids would suppress the Rebellion, they were wrong. Many would suffer this night — and their hatred would grow. The challenge was to focus their emotion, to transmute negative energy into positive.

Morgan watched the fires in and around his house disappear. Activated by the household computer, and fed by the tap tree, his sprinkler system had cut in. He frowned and bit his lip. Possessions could be replaced, but what of Wee Gee? And more importantly, the map which Rahn had entrusted to him. Was it intact? Did the Imperials understand how valuable it was? Morgan ached to return, to check on his home, but knew a trap could be waiting.

Morgan turned, low-crawled off the skyline, and trudged toward the east. Opportunity dwells within disaster. That's what his friend Rahn liked to say — and he hoped it was true.

◆─═◈═─◆

Thrawn received the unenviable task of telling Jerec that while the raid had been successful, the commandos had been unable to find and capture Morgan Katarn. Never one to delay an unpleasant task, Thrawn marched down a gleaming corridor, nodded to the stormtroopers who stood guard outside Jerec's suite, and requested entrance. It came without delay. Having no eyes and no sight, not in the ordinary sense, anyway, Jerec sat in almost total darkness. Only the soft glow provided by the bridge repeaters and light switches lit the room. The lack of illumination was intended to be intimidating, and would have been for anyone but Thrawn, who came from a species that boasted exceedingly good night vision. He waited for Jerec to speak.

"You bring bad news."

Thrawn took note of the fact that the comment came in the form of a statement rather than a question. How did Jerec know? There was no way to tell. "Yes, sir."

"You may continue."

The naval officer delivered his report the same way he delivered *all* reports — without excuse or elaboration. Once Thrawn was finished, thirty seconds elapsed before Jerec spoke. "Was Katarn warned?"

"There's no evidence to support that theory, sir. Lieutenant Brazack believes the subject left the farm on some sort of errand."

"Or *felt* a need to go elsewhere," Jerec mused out loud. "He feels the Force, and even uses it on occasion, but is afraid to reach out and seize his inheritance. 'What if I make a mistake?' he wonders. 'What if I abuse the power?' 'Can I be trusted?' Such silliness is beyond all reckoning! I can feel his presence from orbit. Working, fussing, scheming. All for naught."

Thrawn allowed one eyebrow to rise. In spite of the fact that Jerec went to considerable lengths to hide certain abilities from those above him, chosen subordinates were allowed the occasional glimpse. "Sir . . . yes, sir."

"Of course this holds no interest for you," Jerec sneered. "For you're a being of the physical world, a doer of deeds, a manipulator of objects. Well, O doer of deeds, I will provide you and Lieutenant Brazack an opportunity to redeem yourselves and collect yet another of the commendations you thrive on. Listen carefully, for there is much to do."

⤙ ☰◈☰ ⤚

The room was circular and packed with people. With the exception of an Alliance news team, dispatched to record the proceedings as part of the communications effort required to unite hundreds of sentient species under a single command, the colonists came from all over the district. They were hard men and women, lean of body, used to adversity. Each had been elected to represent at least ten others. They paid strict attention to what was said.

Everything about Skorg Jameson was big, starting with his body and extending to his voice, hand gestures, and movements. He had long shaggy hair that touched the tops of his shoulders, a chest that bulged under his leather jerkin, and boots planted like tree trunks at the center of the hard-packed floor. He stood with his back to a massive fireplace and glared at those around him. "I say the time is now! You saw what happened to Danga, to Katarn, and a dozen more . . . It's time to make a stand and show others what we can do!"

It was a brave speech, and Morgan admired Jameson for making it. Especially in light of the fact that a spy could be present, or a listening device so sophisticated it had escaped the pre-meeting sweep. Of course the words did have a rehearsed quality, and could be part of Jameson's campaign for Sector Leader. There was applause and Morgan allowed it to fade away before speaking his mind.

"I too tire of the pressure, the extortion, and the attacks. That's why it's tempting to look for an opportunity to strike back . . . but at what cost? Yes, some extremely interesting intelligence has come our way. Assuming that citizen Jameson's source of information is correct, and Imperials disguised as Rebels or mercenaries *are* planning to attack the G-Tap."

"Which would force us to buy a fusion plant from the SoroSuub Corporation, and pay taxes to the Empire," Jameson added pointedly.

"Exactly," Morgan said agreeably. "Which is why we sold shares and drilled the shaft to begin with. But what if there's an even deeper purpose? To not only destroy the Tap, but to lure us into a pitched battle and eliminate the Rebel infrastructure on Sulon? Guerilla raids are one thing, but our forces aren't trained or equipped to fight Special Operations commandos. If we lose, we lose more than the G-Tap, we lose Sulon herself."

A good many heads nodded, and voices murmured agreement. Still, only seconds elapsed before one of Jameson's cronies stepped forward to reiterate the big man's point of view. The meeting lasted a full four hours, and by the time it was over, a consensus had been established. The time had come. The Sulon Rebels would defend the G-Tap with everything they had.

The meeting was adjourned and the colonists headed for their vehicles. A highly modified probe droid watched from the cover of some trees. The robot counted the number of people who left, made infrared recordings of their movements, and listened to their parting comments. A summary went to the *Vengeance* seconds after the last conspirator departed and reached Jerec only minutes after that. The Dark Jedi listened to the report and returned to his carefully scented meal. He smiled. Seeds had been sown, crops had flourished, and the harvest was at hand.

⊶ ⊱⊰ ⊷

The upper end of the Geo Thermal, or G-Tap, was located in a sizable cavern chosen both for its relative proximity to the heat trapped in crustal rock formations three kilometers below, and the fact that it was impervious to air attack. A number of prefab structures had been erected around it, including buildings to house the water injection pumps, giant turbines, and adjunct control rooms. Morgan's assignment lay elsewhere, but he paused to catch his breath, and admire what the colonists had accomplished.

The principle was relatively simple and had been put to use on various worlds prior to the rise of the New Order. Crustal rock formations are warmed by volcanic action, an upwelling of magma, and

the natural decay of potassium, thorium, and uranium. By drilling extremely deep wells, the colonists could force water down through carefully engineered cracks, where it could be heated and pumped to the surface. There it would bring isobutane to a boil which would be forced through power-generating turbines. And all this was done without radioactive waste, potentially dangerous technology, or governmental taxes.

That was the idea anyway, and, judging from the nearly completed complex, would soon be a reality. Assuming they could defend it. A voice caused Morgan to turn. "Citizen Katarn? I hoped I'd run into you."

The information officer's name was Candice Ondi. She had brown hair, large intelligent eyes, and an ever-ready smile. In spite of the fact that she was dressed in the ubiquitous gray coveralls that many Rebs wore instead of a uniform, Morgan knew she had a nice figure. He'd have been interested under normal circumstances, but the possibility that many of those around him might be dead soon acted to neutralize any such thoughts.

Ondi traveled with a specially equipped chrome-plated protocol droid called "A-Cee." The robot spoke dozens of languages, had a zoom lens where its right eye sensor should have been, and the ability to record and digitally store more than a thousand hours of audio and video. A-Cee walked with the slightly jerky motion typical of his kind and was engaged in a never-ending search for pickup shots.

Morgan found the possibility that the droid might be recording at any given time more than a little annoying and forced a smile. "Captain Ondi . . . how nice to see you again."

The officer laughed. "I see you're thrilled. Listen, I wanted to thank you for the footage. I'm sorry about what the commandos did to your farm, but a picture's worth a thousand words. Hundreds of thousands of sentients will see it and know what happened here."

A column of Rebels jogged by, weapons held across their chests, headed for the canyon below. That was the most direct approach to the cavern and the one they expected the Imperials to take. The river which was to have fed the G-Tap would provide the stormtroopers with a straight-ahead approach. Morgan turned to Ondi. She dropped a holocam and allowed it to dangle from her wrist. Her eyes were greenish-brown and seemed to see his innermost thoughts. "So, Morgan Katarn, you don't think much of our chances, do you?"

Conscious of his role as a leader, and the importance of good morale, Morgan lied. "On the contrary, Captain Ondi, I think we'll win."

The information officer clearly didn't believe him. She nodded soberly, smiled crookedly, and removed a piece of lint from his shoulder. There was something personal about the gesture, which reminded Morgan of Kyle's mother. He smiled. "Take care of yourself, Captain. No matter what happens today, make sure they see it."

Ondi nodded, a noncom called Morgan's name, and he turned away. They never saw each other again.

In spite of the fact that Major Noda had nominal command of ground forces, he was well aware of the fact that Jerec monitored everything he said and did via comlink transmissions, probe droids, and his own seemingly supernatural powers. The knowledge added to the already considerable amount of stress Noda was under.

Though naturally cautious, Noda was no coward, and had bumped the AT-AT's commanding officer to see the terrain for himself. The walker was over fifteen meters tall and lurched from side to side as it waded upstream. Heavily eroded banks, their tops decorated with hardy-looking bushes, rose to either side.

A great deal of time and energy had been spent painting Rebel insignia on the ATs. Noda considered such efforts a waste of time. After all, the very notion that the Rebels could capture such powerful weapons and turn them against their owners was absurd. Still, orders were orders, and the charade would continue.

The pilot, who had spent most of the last three days in an AT-AT simulator preparing for this precise moment, handled the current with ease. Water swirled white around the machine's massive legs and raced downstream. A bend obscured the river ahead and Noda watched as the second of two AT-STs disappeared behind it. There was an explosion, smoke boiled up from the point the walkers should be, and the battle began.

Although Morgan didn't actually see the missile hit the AT-ST, he heard the comlink chatter that described it, and saw the smoke boil up from the canyon. In spite of his position as a resistance leader and respected member of the community, Morgan had relatively little military expertise. That's why he'd been relegated to what the Rebels commonly referred to as the "back door," the flat area above the cavern, which was accessed via an easily defended passageway that wound down through a series of caves and vaults and into the main chamber.

Which explained why the twenty-six soldiers under Morgan's command were teenagers or senior citizens. They cheered as the walker exploded and were still celebrating when a woman named Crowley touched his arm. She'd been a Master Sergeant in the Republic's Army and was the only member of his platoon with real combat experience. "Look, Morgan! Coming out of the sun!"

Morgan pulled his visor into place and turned towards the sun. The vessel was too far away for a positive ID — but the Rebel *knew* what it was . . . The same Corellian-built freighter that had attacked his farm. Loaded with commandos and headed his way. He switched to the platoon frequency and warned his troops. "There's an Imperial assault ship headed in. Don't be fooled by the Rebel markings. Everyone but the missile team into the passageway. Trol . . . Jen . . . kill that ship before it lands."

"Gotcha!" Trol said enthusiastically. "Don't worry, Morgan — the ship is toast. Come on, Jen — load my tube."

The teenagers took up a position behind some boulders as the rest of the platoon scurried for the protection of the passageway. Trol, his eyes on the heads up display projected on the inside surface of his visor, watched the ship grow larger. The launch tube rested on his right shoulder. The trick was to wait, thereby increasing the chance of a hit, but not *too* long since the SLM needed time to arm itself. That's where old man Danga had gone wrong. Trol was determined to get it right.

—+— ⧩◆⧨ —+—

Vester fired retros, lit his repulsors, and allowed the bow to rise as the ship sank. That blocked his view of the ground but put more metal between him and whatever the groundies chose to send his way. It was a trick that infantry officers frowned on since it exposed the ship's belly to more enemy fire.

Brazack felt the deck tilt, knew what Vester was doing, and swore under his breath. This wasn't the time or place to deal with the pilot, but later, after the battle was over, he would find the little creep and teach him a lesson.

—+— ⧩◆⧨ —+—

Trol heard a soft beeping sound through his ear plug, checked to make sure the crosshairs were properly centered on the underside of the ship, and pressed the firing stud. The tube lurched as the SLM raced upwards, hit the freighter dead on, and exploded. The ship lurched, slipped sideways, and steadied under Vester's hands. The Corellian shields, built to withstand the rigors of space combat, held.

Trol felt a vague uneasiness in the pit of his stomach, waited for Jen to shove a second SLM into the tube, and fired again. The missile had barely left the launcher when the laser beam found it. Trol, Jen, and the boulders they had been hiding behind vanished in a flash of light.

Morgan winced, thought about their families, and winced again. Then the freighter was down, commandos disguised as rebels were pouring out of its belly, and lasers were probing the rocks. Morgan fired and had the satisfaction of seeing an Imperial fall. Then it was time to pull back, take up a position behind the first of many prepre-pared rock barricades, and fight the first of what would turn out to be a long series of delaying actions.

⤜✦⤛

The Rebels fought well, much better than Jerec, Thrawn, Noda, or Brazack thought they could or would, but the result was inevitable. Just as Morgan and his steadily diminishing team were driven inex-orably down, the rest of the Rebel force, those who had confronted Noda down in the canyon, were forced up and back. The Imperials paid a bloody price for each and every foot of ground they gained, but there were more of them and they were better trained. Finally, after four hours of intense combat, both contingents of stormtroopers met in the main chamber. The ensuing fight was brief and more than a lit-tle one-sided.

Only thirty-seven colonists were left by that time. Those who could stand were lined up in front of the nearly completed G-Tap and sorted according to instructions issued by Jerec. Major Noda consulted a data pad as he inspected each face. Information provided by Jerec's agents combined with data compiled by probe droids had been used to create detailed profiles. Most of the Rebels would be put to death. A few, those who held leadership positions, would be held for interrogation.

Morgan Katarn had been wounded two hours before. He swayed slightly as Major Noda made his way down the line. The Rebel leader harbored no illusions. He knew what awaited him and felt nothing but sadness, not for himself, but for the young people whose lives had barely begun.

Noda's face was little more than a blur when it appeared in front of him. Morgan had the vague impression of black hair, almond-shaped eyes, and high cheekbones. The voice was brusque and unemotional. "Jerec wants this one — take him to the shuttle." Hands grabbed

Morgan's arms; he struggled to free himself, and fell as vertigo pulled him down.

⊷ ⊱☰◈☰⊰ ⊶

A noncom slapped Morgan across the face while a medic injected something into his arm. Whatever it was cleared the cobwebs and left him unnaturally alert. So much so that he could see nearly microscopic differences between hull rivets, hear air as it passed through the recycling ducts, and feel drops of sweat as they popped through the surface of his skin. All for what? So he could feel pain more acutely — and tell them what they wanted to know.

Morgan felt the toes of his boots bump over durasteel hull plating as the stormtroopers dragged him into the interrogation chamber and allowed him to fall. He was admiring the precision with which the construction droids had mated two of the floor plates when a pair of shiny black boots appeared in front of his face. They frightened him and he wasn't sure why.

Hands grabbed Morgan under the armpits and lifted him to his feet. Black tattoos covered the lower portion of the face before him. The drugs in his bloodstream brought them to life. They slithered back and forth. He searched for his tormentor's eyes, for the pathway to his spirit, and found nothing but blackness. The man's words were soft and smelled of mint. This was the one known as Jerec. Morgan had heard of him.

"Citizen Katarn — how nice to see you. Which would you prefer? A long, painful conversation? Or something brief and to the point? I would choose the second, less difficult path if I were in your position."

Morgan's mouth felt desert dry. He worked his mouth as if preparing to speak, mustered some saliva, and aimed for Jerec's face. The liquid fell woefully short and splattered on the other man's boots. Jerec shook his head mockingly. "How disappointing. I expected more from someone of your reputation. A snappy reply, a Rebel slogan, or heroic silence. Ah, well, it's always better to overestimate one's opponents than the other way around. Now tell me, who do you take orders from, and where are they?"

Morgan felt his heart pound against his chest. So that was it. Jerec hoped to start at the bottom and work his way up through the Rebel chain of command. Kill the leaders and you kill the revolution. It was as simple as that. He thought about Kyle, wished he'd been allowed to see him one last time, and willed himself to die. It didn't work. His mouth was still dry and words felt unwieldy. "A Gamorrean princess

27

delivers my orders every morning and lives under my barn."

Jerec fingered the baton-shaped vibroblade. Energy sizzled. The stink of ozone filled the air.

Morgan thought about Kyle and the man he hoped his son would be. There was an explosion of light, his wife's face, and a feeling of peace.

Jerec heard Morgan's head thump against the deck, found the vibroblade's off switch, and restored the device to his belt. "Many years ago I had the somewhat dubious pleasure of passing through Sulon's spaceport. A plain, rather spartan facility, as I recall — has it changed?"

A noncom, the most senior trooper present, snapped to attention. He was terrified and unable to conceal it. "Sir! No, sir!"

"Excellent. That being the case I would like to add a little color to the place. Install this head where all may see and take inspiration from it. In the meantime, I want the following message sent to Emperor Palpatine: 'Sulon has been pacified. Your obedient servant, Jerec.'"

CHAPTER 2

Kyle Katarn didn't want to die. Not for the Emperor, not for the Empire, and not for anyone else. The realization brought color to his cheeks and Kyle was grateful for the glossy white armor that protected his body and concealed his features. The men around him were *real* stormtroopers and, if it weren't for his helmet, would have seen the fear in his eyes.

Of course that's what the Omega Exercise was for — to test cadets in battle and see what they were made of. Those who completed their missions with a satisfactory score would receive their commissions and graduate from the Imperial Military Academy at Cliffside on Carida. Failures like Kyle would serve in the ranks. An honorable occupation for anyone but a cadet. Maybe the Rebels would kill him *before* he could embarrass himself. A rather unusual wish for a cadet to make.

A pair of TIE fighters made the third of three consecutive runs, declared the asteroid "clean," and vectored away. The assault boat, just one of hundreds of support craft carried aboard the Star Destroyer *Imperator*, shuddered slightly and dumped speed as the pilot fired his retros. It required skill to match velocities with an asteroid and AX-456 was no exception. Maybe the pixel pixies back on the ship knew why the Rebs chose 456 for their relay station and maybe not. Not that it mattered much. A ride is a ride — and the pilot went where they told him to.

The sun broke over the planetoid's horizon and activated the polarizing filter in the pilot's face mask. He checked course and speed, pushed the nose down, and chinned the intercom. "We are three — repeat three — to dirt. Check life support and prepare for insertion."

Frightened though Kyle was, he'd been trained for this moment, and reacted without thinking. "Systems check — top down. Katarn — green."

The names came in order, starting with his second in command, Sergeant Major Hong, followed by the members of squads one, two, and three. Everything checked, leaving the entire outfit "green and clean."

Kyle tried to report, heard his voice crack, and tried again. "Cadet Leader Katarn here — all systems green. Ready for insertion."

"Roger that," the pilot replied matter-of-factly. "Atmospheric decompression commencing now. Thirty to dirt."

Kyle chinned the command freq and gave the appropriate orders. "Decomp underway. Thirty to dirt. Lock and load."

The stormtroopers sat on bench-style seats with their backs to the bulkheads. They brought their assault weapons to the vertical position, aligned power paks with receiver slots, and shoved them into place. Forgetting to do so was the kind of thing greenies did and got killed for.

Kyle checked to ensure that his power source was "locked," verified the "full load" reading, and released the safety. The cadet carried a side arm as well. But he knew better than to check it. Not with fifteen seconds remaining.

Time seemed to slow. Lead filled his stomach and he was unexplainably sleepy. What was the quote? The one carved into the mantel above the fireplace in Cliffside's ceremonial dining room? Something about how cowards die a thousand deaths . . . ? Then, before Kyle could count how many times he had died during the last few hours, the assault boat hit. It bounced once, twice, and stuck. Like the first landings he had attempted, only better.

The port and starboard hatches opened and the squad leaders led their men into hard vacuum. Hong stood between the hatches with his back to the cockpit. He had a small body and a big voice. "Move it, move it, move it! What the heck are you waiting for, Briggs? An engraved invitation? Get out there and kill some Rebels!"

Kyle felt an ice-cold hand grab hold of his stomach, forced himself to stand, and wondered when the fighting would start. The Rebs should have reacted by now, should have opened fire with everything they had, but nothing had happened. Why? Or, better yet, why not? Maybe the rumors were true. Maybe the optimists were right for a change. Maybe ninety percent of senior missions were walkovers.

The hand released his stomach for a moment and Kyle shuffled towards the bow. Gravity was tenuous at best, and even though the entire platoon had spent two days in a prestrike acclimation tank, it took time to adjust. Hong snapped to attention. "Troops deployed, sir — no sign of opposition."

Kyle wondered what was taking place behind the dark gray lenses and white armor. How much did Hong know? Did he have any idea how frightened his commanding officer was? How close to crumbling? There was no way to tell. But one thing was for sure, Hong's opinion would weigh heavily when his final score was tallied. Assuming he got that far . . . Kyle knew the proper response and delivered it in the calm, matter-of-fact style favored by Cliffside's instructors. "Thank you, Sergeant Major. Let's get on with it."

"Yes, sir."

Kyle stepped out of the hatch first, followed by Hong. Dust fountained up around his boots and fell in slow motion. The ground was rugged and almost universally gray. Impact craters marked the spots where meteorites had slammed into the surface. They provided excellent cover and the troopers took advantage of it. The assault boat crouched on a rise where it could lift quickly — or offer fire support if called upon to do so. The whole thing looked like a text-book scenario, which added to Kyle's confidence. Maybe, just maybe, he would survive.

Kyle, more from curiosity than bravado, remained standing. The electrobinoculars provided magnification and range as he scanned the enemy base. The installations included a comm dish, a boxlike structure, and a landing pad. They had a raw, improvised look. The pre-mission simulation had portrayed the constructs as only fifty-percent complete, but that data was two weeks old, and the Rebs had been busy since then.

The purpose of the facility, and others like it, was a matter of conjecture. Intel's best guess was that the Rebs were trying to establish a network of relay stations that could pass intelligence and psyprop broadcasts from one sector to another. All part of the battle for the hearts and minds of the civilian population.

Not that it made a heck of a lot of difference. Whatever the purpose, Kyle knew that what he saw on the surface didn't say much about the rest of the complex. No, based on the intelligence gathered by an Imperial probe droid, there might be as many as a hundred Rebs living and working beneath the surface. Especially during the construction phase. So where were they? Was the situation a walkover or a trap? He turned to Hong. "Send the scouts. Tell them to keep a sharp eye out. This place is too darned quiet."

Hong, who privately agreed, thanked the gods of war for a greenie who had some brains, and gave the necessary orders. "Dobbs, Trang, Sutu . . . take a look. Somebody built that dish — find 'em."

The scouts, each from a different squad, cursed their rotten luck and low-crawled forward. Ribbons of slowly falling dust spiraled up around them and marked their progress. They knew that made them easy meat for a sniper, had there been one to shoot at them.

Kyle scanned the area. The stars were smears of distant light. The crags, those that had survived, stood as they had for thousands of years. In spite of the fact that everything looked normal — it didn't *feel* normal — and that was what bothered him. Both because he'd been trained to make fact-based decisions, and because the feeling was so strong. Someone, something, was watching. That's the way it felt. But the reports said otherwise.

"Trang — lots of tracks — nothing else. Over."

"Dobbs — ditto. Over."

"Sutu — looks clear. Over."

The fear was back and Kyle swallowed the lump that had formed in his throat. "Sergeant Major — the second squad will blow the lock, one will provide cover, and three will follow me."

Hong nodded. "Yes, sir. You heard the Cadet Leader, Sergeant Morley. Let's get cracking."

Based on information provided by the probe droid, demolitions charges had been prepared in advance. They had been placed and were ready for detonation by the time Kyle arrived.

The entry was a massive affair built to withstand a meteor hit. Two magnetic demo charges had been attached to the metal faceplate. It was a standard prefab affair set into quick-drying permacrete and controlled via numeric key pad. The straight-ahead "here-I-am" vid pickup located next to the frame had been blinded with spray seal, as had the tiny pinhead lens hidden into the right-hand sidewall. Very sneaky. How many more existed? And where were they located?

Morley spoke with his characteristic drawl. "She's ready to blow, sir."

Kyle looked around. The troopers assumed it was one last check prior to giving the order, but he knew the action for what it *really* was. A search for an excuse, *any* excuse, to scrub the mission. None presented itself. The hand took hold of Kyle's stomach, sweat prickled his skin, and his voice sounded thick. "Take cover — detonate on my command."

The stormtroopers pulled back and found cover. Kyle stepped around the corner of the building, took a deep breath, and gave the order. "Now."

Morley triggered the remote and an eruption of dust signaled that the charges had been detonated. This was the moment Kyle had been

dreading, when he would step through the hatch and take a blaster bolt in the chest. He wanted to speak, wanted to say something, but couldn't find the words. His movements were jerky, like those of the toy soldiers his father had fashioned for him. Miniature robots that marched this way and that, saluted when they saw him, and tripped over irregularities in the workshop floor.

Suddenly, without remembering how he had arrived there, Kyle was inside the hatch. He had no more than entered when Morley brushed past him, slapped another charge against the inside door, and hollered "Duck!" The "sir" was an obvious afterthought.

The inner charges exploded with a flash of light. Morley jumped up, shoved the heavily damaged slab of metal to one side, and swore as a blaster bolt bounced off his reflective armor. An ambush? Kyle's worst fears had been realized. A wave of self-pity swept over him. He had joined to get an education, not die on some asteroid. It wasn't fair. Or was it? After all, no one had forced him to attend the Academy, he had chosen to do so — and the men were waiting for an order. Four years of hard, rigorous training kicked in. "Contact! Two grenades — one concussion — one high-explosive."

The words were no more than out of Kyle's mouth than two grenades sailed through the door, exploded, and threw shrapnel in every direction. Morley passed through the hole first, followed by Kyle, Hong, and the members of squad two. Suddenly, Kyle was faced with the harsh reality of what war does to people. He swallowed to keep his breakfast down and looked ahead.

The next lock, a backup in case a meteorite destroyed the first one, opened automatically. Kyle entered ready to fire. The second door was closed and there was little doubt as to what waited on the other side. "Second squad? Heavy weapons to the front — pack the lock."

Two stormtroopers, both armed with blaster cannons and the power modules necessary to operate them, took up positions in front of the door. Ten additional troopers filled in behind. Hong slapped a button and the door cycled shut. Kyle clenched his teeth. "First rank, prepare to fire — second, third, and fourth ranks, rifle salute."

The rifle salute, normally rendered to officers while under arms, forced the second, third, and fourth ranks to hold their weapons in the vertical position and guarded against an accidental discharge.

The hatch slid open, the first rank fired, and reeled as the fire storm hit them. The first line of stormtroopers died within a matter of seconds, quickly followed by at least half of the second. Not without cost, however, since there was little to no cover in the room beyond, and the Rebels were exposed.

Kyle felt anger replace the fear that had very nearly paralyzed him, fired his weapon, and yelled encouragement. "Come on, men! Take them out!"

Kyle stepped out of the lock and shot a woman through the chest. She fell in slow motion and the cadet felt shock course through his body. This was a person, not a target — and the realization froze him in place. He felt a terrible sense of remorse, and stood frozen while Morley clutched his faceplate and fell over backwards.

The Rebel who killed Morley was little more than a boy, but he was old enough to take a life, and Kyle shot him through the chest. The words came from deep within and boomed through the command channel. If his men thought them strange they had no opportunity to comment on the matter. "Morley was a person, too!"

The battle raged on. The Rebs were a diverse bunch. Kyle saw men, women, and a scattering of aliens, some of which he recognized and some he didn't. They came in all colors, shapes, and sizes and fought with weapons as varied as they were. Kyle saw blasters old and new, plus some low-velocity projectile weapons, and at least one pre-Empire vibroaxe of the sort used to board enemy starships. It was an ugly weapon and cut through Imperial armor as if it were constructed from paper. Hong shot the axeman through the head, shot him a second time just to make sure, and led the charge that secured the room and fifty feet of passageway.

With that accomplished, Kyle took a moment to assess the situation. A quick count revealed that the platoon had suffered thirty percent casualties, with the second squad being nearly all killed, the third having lost two men, and the first, which had passed through the locks last, almost untouched. So much for the walkover theory. If this was the Academy's idea of easy, it was a wonder that anyone survived to graduate.

A hand touched Kyle's arm. He turned to find a medic standing beside him. He had a blaster burn along one side of his helmet and other people's blood on his arms. "How 'bout the Rebs, sir? Give 'em aid or put 'em out of their misery?"

Kyle knew what ninety-nine percent of his fellow officers would say: put them out of their misery. He couldn't bring himself to give the order though — not in cold blood. He looked around. The floor was littered with bodies. "Our people come first, the Rebels after that. Military intelligence will want to interrogate the prisoners."

The medic nodded respectfully and hurried off to inform his team. Hong appeared, removed his helmet, and wiped the perspiration from his forehead. Hong wore his hair high and tight but allowed himself a carefully tended mustache. If he was worried he gave no sign of it. Kyle wasn't absolutely sure, but he thought he saw respect in the other man's eyes, and felt some pride trickle into his chest. He realized that in spite of the fact that the fear remained crouched in his belly, *he* controlled *it*, instead of the other way around. The cadet removed his helmet and held it in the crook of his arm.

"So, Sergeant Major, our instructors taught us that when things go south, and we need advice, we should ask for it. What do you think? Should we pull out? Or press ahead?"

Hong's already high estimation of the young officer's ability went up a notch. He knew from sad experience that nine out of ten of Kyle's peers would have been too proud to ask for advice. "I say we call for reinforcements, then press ahead, sir. The Rebs have got to be hurting, and I'd hate to use up even more lives breaking in all over again."

The advice made sense and served to validate Kyle's instincts. He nodded, chose the correct tac frequency, and spoke into his wrist com. "C-1 to R-1. Over."

He heard the crackle of static followed by the pilot's voice. The signal was scrambled in both directions. "R-1 here — go. Over."

"I need a sitrep, One — any activity out there? Over."

"The Rebs sent some coded comm traffic, C-1 — and I've got a feeling they have backup on the way. Over."

Kyle winced at his own stupidity. He'd been so scared, so stupid, that he'd forgotten the comlink. "Grease the antenna, R-1 — and tell the *Imperator* to send some reinforcements. We took thirty percent casualties getting into this place, and there's no end in sight. Acknowledge. Over."

"Burn the link and call for backup," the pilot said calmly. "Got it. Hang in there, C-1. Out."

Kyle looked at Hong. "All right, Sergeant Major. Enough goofing off. Move 'em out."

Hong grinned, popped a salute, and did an about-face. "Okay, people, you heard the Cadet Leader, let's finish what we started. First squad first, third squad second, second squad hold." The few surviving members of the second squad, most of whom were wounded, watched dully as their comrades entered a large underground passageway. Three heavily armed troopers led the phalanx, with Kyle and Hong immediately behind.

The corridor was wide enough to accommodate heavy equipment, and the walls bore the marks left by the mole miner used to create it, plus some not very original graffiti regarding the Emperor. Blood left by the wounded and two widely separated bodies gave mute testimony to the fact that the Rebels had suffered heavy casualties as well.

Side tunnels branched left and right. Some of them could accommodate humans, while many couldn't. The function of the passageways wasn't clear, and Kyle didn't care, as long as the Rebels didn't launch an attack from one of them. He sent scouts down the larger ones and waited for the all clear before continuing on. A quiet trip mostly, the silence broken only by their footsteps and the sound of his own breathing.

So it went for a kilometer or so, until the ground shook, and Kyle heard a loud cracking sound through his external comlink. It came from behind and the cadet turned in time to see the tunnel collapse.

Suddenly, without knowing *how* he knew, Kyle glimpsed the future. Where the well-lit corridor had been he saw only darkness and the flash of energy weapons. The words tumbled out of his mouth. "Hit the dirt! Low-crawl forward!"

The orders made no apparent sense, but if the Imperial stormtroopers knew anything, it was how to obey orders, and they did so to a man. Kyle's vision, and the resulting order, saved many of their lives.

The moment the lights went out, the Rebels opened fire through hastily drilled holes. The fire, most of which passed over the stormtroopers' heads, splashed against the opposite wall. Kyle, knowing a frontal attack was on the way, elbowed forward. They needed cover, *any* kind of cover, if they hoped to survive. His helmet light wobbled across the back end of a much-abused crawler, and the alternating black and yellow stripes that covered the bumper. "Take cover behind the crawler! Prepare to engage!"

The words were no sooner out of Kyle's mouth than the Rebels dropped grenades through the weapon apertures. The explosions came two seconds apart and were followed by the screams of wounded men. Hong, his voice harsh, remonstrated those who cried out. "The tac frequency is intended for verbal communication. Use it that way."

It seemed as if the mission had turned into an unending nightmare, where everything that *could* happen *did* happen, and was immediately followed by something even worse.

The lights flashed on and the stormtroopers fired as a wall-to-wall line of droids rolled, hopped, glided, and lurched in their direction. Kyle recognized a pair of heavy-duty construction droids, a spidery freight loader, two A-types, and a forlorn R2 unit, all condemned to an electromechanical suicide mission. None of the machines were armed, or programmed for combat, but they were bulky and provided cover for the Rebels behind them.

Blaster bolts flashed out and struck stormtroopers where they lay.

One of them tried to stand and staggered as the Rebs cut him down. The range was short, too short to fire grenades safely, but Kyle saw no alternative. "Grenades! Front and rear."

The robots staggered and came apart as the grenades exploded around them. A stormtrooper's head flew off. Blood sprayed upward. No longer protected, the Rebels fired, and backed away. Furious, the surviving stormtroopers stood and met fire with fire. The Rebs turned and ran. The Imperials continued to fire. The sight made Kyle sick, and he was just about to order the firing to stop when the last man fell. His body skidded all the way to the durasteel door.

Kyle had given up all hope of capturing the facility. He had to focus on salvaging what remained of his first command. And there wasn't much to save. The platoon was down to Sergeant Major Hong, twelve effectives, and two walking wounded. A retreat was unrealistic. To backtrack they'd have to pass the weapons slots, and, assuming they made it all the way to the cave-in, tons of rock blocked the way. No, their single remaining hope was to blow the door, and search for another way out. Unless reinforcements had arrived — which would change everything.

Kyle called R-1, heard nothing but static, and tried again. Same result. Maybe the additional thickness of rock had blocked his signal, maybe the assault boat had been forced to leave, or maybe just about anything. It hardly mattered. All he could do was work with the information at hand and hope for the best.

Kyle looked at Hong. "There's no going back, Sergeant Major. Tell the men to scavenge for power paks — drag the droids forward — and blow the door."

Hong nodded soberly. "Yes, sir. They're gonna be waiting for us, sir."

Kyle nodded as he surveyed the rough-hewn walls, the blood-splattered floor, and the remains of his first command. The strange part was that the mission had been far worse than even his worst imaginings — yet the fear had disappeared.

Kyle looked around and saw that his men had taken up positions to either side of the door, while Corporal Givens placed a magnetic demo charge against the control panel. Givens made one last adjustment to the charge and turned. "Any time, sir."

Kyle nodded. "Thank you, Givens. Spread out, men, stay low, and prepare to fire. They'll be waiting for us. And remember — make every shot count. Power paks are getting hard to come by."

Except for the droids small enough to drag forward, there wasn't a whole lot of cover in the passageway. Still, the Imperials took advantage of what there was, and Kyle gave the order. The blast blew the control panel out of the wall. Sparks arced, an electrical fire started, and the door whirred open.

The Rebs were waiting all right, and opened up with everything they had. A barricade of sorts had been erected and the usual odd assortment of men, women, and aliens had taken refuge behind a makeshift wall of cargo modules, cable reels, and furniture.

Kyle noticed as he aimed and fired that these particular Rebels seemed less disciplined than those they had encountered before. Some had a tendency to fire in a wild, undisciplined manner, others carried second-rate weapons, and at least two or three were frozen in place.

Were they noncombatants then? Men and women who had been pressed into service out of desperation? They had numbers on their side, however, plus much better cover. Three of his troopers died and the rest moved forward. The Rebels held for a moment, wavered in the face of incoming fire, and broke.

The stormtroopers continued to fire and Kyle knew he couldn't allow a massacre. His voice boomed over the command channel. "That's enough — hold your fire."

Hong turned in Kyle's direction. Even though he couldn't see the noncom's expression, the cadet could sense the frown on his face. Kyle found an excuse and ran it out. "We need to conserve our ammo, Sergeant Major. Most of the stuff the Rebs left won't do us any good. Come to think of it — let's use *their* oxygen for a while."

Hong nodded and turned away. Kyle gave a sigh of relief, waved the men forward, and followed the handwritten signs. They read "Comm Center" and led him past what smelled like a cafeteria, a series of cavelike storage rooms, down a businesslike corridor. The rough-hewn walls supported an electronic message board and a hodge-podge of printouts. One announced a birthday party for someone named Blim Shahar, and another cautioned base personnel to conserve on water.

Kyle surprised himself by having the presence of mind to scan the bulletins with the tiny battle holocam built into his helmet. The military intelligence geeks would be thrilled, and, in the unlikely event that he survived, the instructors would award him some extra mission points. Collateral documentation was just one of the thousand things an infantry officer was supposed to remember and take care of.

A maintenance droid chose that particular moment to poke its nose out of a side passage, saw the Imperials, and gave a squeak of alarm. The droid had already engaged reverse gear, and was in the process of backing away when an energy bolt splashed the rock behind it. Hong's voice dripped with sarcasm. "Thanks, Dendu. You wasted a shot *and* missed the target. The Emperor would be proud."

A pair of light-duty doors blocked the way. They rolled into the walls at Kyle's approach. He prepared to fire but saw nothing more threatening than some gray equipment racks. Moving cautiously, weapons at the ready, the troopers entered the room, turned to the right, and were confronted by an amazing sight.

The Rebels, about fifteen or twenty of them, stood with their backs to a wall full of monitors and related communications gear with their hands in the air. Kyle, who was ready for anything but a surrender, struggled to cope. He checked to make sure the Rebs were covered, removed his helmet, and used his forearm to smear the sweat across his brow. What would he do with prisoners? They outnumbered his team and would be difficult to herd around. No, the more expedient solution was to kill them, trash the control room, and get out while the getting was good. Especially with more Rebels on the way.

As Kyle considered the feasibility of what amounted to mass murder, his eyes drifted across an oval-shaped face. Something, he would never know exactly what, caught his attention. The girl was about his age, perhaps a little younger, dressed in a flight suit. She had dark brown eyes that matched the color of her hair and seemed to draw him in. It was peaceful there, yet centered, as if her whole being was focused on something he couldn't see.

At that precise moment, a spark leapt the gap between them, and she, like the first person he had killed, crossed the line from variable to person. Not only that — Kyle knew she had experienced something as well. He could tell from the way her eyes widened. He felt his heart beat a tiny bit faster. He knew then that he couldn't kill this young woman — or the others, either.

Sergeant Major Hong brought Kyle back to the present. His voice came over the command frequency. "Look! Up on that monitor, sir! I don't know who that ship belongs to, but it ain't one of ours. Let's grease the Rebs and get the heck out of here!"

Kyle looked, saw a freighter settle into place, and watched dust shoot upward as a ramp touched the ground. It didn't take a genius to know that Reb reinforcements were on the way. His voice was surprisingly strong, and because his helmet was off, the prisoners heard it too. "Negative on greasing the Rebs, Sergeant Major. There's been enough killing today."

Hong turned. Even though the cadet couldn't see his eyes through the visor, he could feel their intensity. The voice was like steel. "With all due respect, *sir*, the Rebs wasted two-thirds of *your* command, and will kill even more of our troops if you let them go."

Kyle shook his head. "The answer is no. You heard my orders, carry them out."

Hong nodded stiffly. "Yes, sir. Under protest, sir. Jonsey, pull the memory mods from the transmitters, Haku, set some charges. We don't have much time."

Kyle looked at the monitor, saw space-suited Rebs flooding out of the freighter's cargo hatch, and wondered how R-1 had fared. Had the assault boat escaped? Were Imperial reinforcements on the way? The questions were academic as far as he was concerned. If he survived the next few hours — and that was a mighty big *if* — he'd be court-martialed for allowing the Rebs to live. A punishment he very likely deserved.

Kyle looked at the girl, saw the thanks in her eyes, and nodded. She at least was well worth saving. The helmet smelled of sweat as he pulled it over his head. "All right, men, clear the room, and let's find a place to hole up. Reinforcements are on the way."

Kyle had no idea if his words were true. But he knew the men needed to hear them. He waved the Rebs to the far end of the room, waited for his team to back out through the door, and followed. The moment they were clear, he yelled "Detonate the charges! Follow me!" and sprinted down the hall. He felt rather than heard the explosions. The Rebs had plenty of time to take cover and he hoped they had. Especially the girl.

For reasons he wasn't entirely sure of, Kyle had identified the cafeteria as the best place to hole up. He skidded to a stop, stuck his head around the door, and confirmed the room was empty. "All right, men, stack some furniture in front of that door, and check for exits. It's time for lunch."

The joke got a chuckle as Kyle had hoped that it would, the stormtroopers stacked tables against the door, and secured the air-conditioning ducts. Once that was accomplished, he allowed them to take turns ransacking the coolers, and offered an overnight pass to the trooper who made the most outrageous sandwich.

They even made one for Kyle, and the Cadet Leader had removed his helmet to eat it when a crawler-mounted drill bit broke through the back wall. Kyle barely had time to pull his helmet back on before Rebs poured through the hole and opened fire on the stormtroopers. Hong and four or five more died within the first five seconds of combat. Kyle swore, turned, and fired. Something hit his helmet, he fell, and darkness rose all around him.

CHAPTER 3

Kyle walked out through the main entrance of the hospital, blinked in the harsh sunlight produced by Carida's sun, and returned an enlisted man's salute. Stone neks crouched to either side of the entryway, each large enough to swallow an assault boat, symbolic of the Empire's strength. He started down the long flight of stairs. A metal railing separated downward-bound pedestrians from those coming up. Consistent with the Emperor's disdain for other sentient species, and his not-so-subtle discrimination against women, most were both human and male.

The Imperial Military Training Base on Carida was home to more than one hundred and fifty thousand recruits, cadets, and instructors. The Military Academy, also known as Cliffside due to the dropoff along the east side of the parade ground, took up less than one-tenth of the sprawling base, but produced a high percentage of the Empire's officer corps.

The hospital, which had been busy to begin with, was even more so thanks to the steady trickle of casualties from missions like Kyle's. The cadet fell in behind some med techs and was halfway to the quad when someone hollered his name and grabbed his arm.

The voice had a nasal quality. It had followed him nearly every day of the last four years. It belonged to Nathan Donar III, eldest son to Governor Donar II, and a real pain in the posterior. Beady brown eyes regarded Kyle from above a long thin nose. They were filled with false bonhomie. "Rimmer! How's the noggin? Good to see you up and around!"

Kyle pulled his arm free, waved an acknowledgment, and continued on his way. Faces blurred as more congratulations came his way. It seemed as if everyone had heard the story. There were various versions but all of them had common elements: The Cadet Leader had encountered unexpectedly heavy opposition, and, rather than turn back as any normal person would do, had fought his way through the corridors of a major Rebel installation, killing no less than four hundred and thirty-six insurrectionists and disabling an important communications installation. All of which Kyle knew to be a greatly exaggerated account of what actually happened. And the last part of the story he only knew secondhand.

It seemed that two Rebel ships had arrived shortly after he'd been knocked unconscious, loaded the surviving staff, and lifted off. The first vessel made it, but the second fell victim to reinforcements summoned by R-1, and was completely destroyed. A force of heavily armed commandos had swept through the Rebel base and found Kyle and the six remaining members of his original force. All were wounded and crouched behind a hastily built barricade. To Kyle, this seemed a clear indication of his failure. No one would listen to his objections, however, least of all the great General Mohc, who had appeared at Kyle's bedside two days ago and commended the cadet for his bravery.

Later that evening, over dinner with Jerec, Mohc mentioned the young cadet's exploits. Jerec, his empty eye sockets hidden behind a band of black, looked up from his half-cooked meat. He couldn't see what the meal looked like but could smell the residue of blood. "I knew the boy's father. His life was wasted. Perhaps the boy will be different. I'd like to meet him."

Mohc nodded, remembered that his guest was blind, and replied out loud. "It shall be as you say."

Jerec, who saw more than Mohc could imagine, smiled and dabbed at his lips. The meal was delicious.

Kyle, who had no knowledge that such deliberations had taken place, left the stairs. The large open area in front of him was referred to as "the quad" on the interactive maps issued to visitors, but the cadets called it "the grinder." How many hours — how many days — had he spent marching back and forth across these acres of fused stone? He wasn't sure. The main thing he remembered was the mind-bending fatigue that stemmed from endless physical training, long hours of study, and intentional sleep deprivation. All that was behind him now, with graduation only hours away.

The thought brought guilt, but he pushed it away. No one else cared about the truth. Why should he?

Kyle took the most direct route across the grinder, a path that took

him through the shadow cast by a heroic statue of Emperor Palpatine.

A column of underclassmen double timed through the space in front of Kyle and their leader snapped a salute in the senior's direction. He returned it, and in doing so, felt inexplicably happy. Somehow, against all odds, he had survived the mission and the commission would be his. His father would be proud, he would find a way to make up for his past mistakes, and everything would be fine. The thought put a spring in his step and Kyle quick marched toward the dorms.

Behind the cadet, so high up that the movement was lost from the ground, a pair of electromechanical eyes blinked open and added one more image to the hundreds available on the video mosaic that filled an entire wall of the Commandant's underground office. The cadets were a mischievous lot. It was a good idea to keep an eye on them.

⊶⊷ ⊟◆⊟ ⊶⊷

Graduation day dawned bright and cold. Light streamed in through the curtainless windows and splashed across the synthetic floor. Kyle rolled out of bed, stretched, yawned, realized that the bad dreams had taken the night off, and took pleasure in the fact that his vision was clear.

Meck Odom, Kyle's roommate, was still asleep. Kyle grinned, said, "Hey dinko breath! Time to get up!" and kicked the other cadet's rack. Having elicited the usual response, an oath accompanied by a flying pillow, Kyle headed for the shower. He, like those he met in the hall, was in a jubilant mood. An inspection, another march in the hot sun, and some boring speeches. That was all that stood between them and the commissions they had worked so hard to achieve.

The next few hours were consumed by an orgy of pressing, dressing, and shining, all followed by a preinspection inspection, and a lecture on deportment. Once that was out of the way, the cadets assembled in front of their dorm and marched to the quad.

A team of maintenance workers, freshmen, and droids had worked through the night to erect temporary grandstands, pylons from which gaily colored pennants flew, along with all manner of bunting, battle flags, and regimental heraldry. It made an impressive and heart stirring sight, as did the endless ranks of infantry, plus the company of Imperial walkers, which included four gigantic AT-ATs, and four of the smaller but no less intimidating AT-STs.

Yes, the sight of all that military might, combined with Palpatine's statue, the marches played by the Regimental Band, and the roar produced by wave after wave of rooftop-skimming TIE fighters made each cadet's spine a tiny bit straighter, brought smiles to the faces of parents fortunate enough, and wealthy enough, to attend in person, and, when played as part of the heavily censored evening news, would serve to reassure the billions of Imperial citizens who, either willingly or unwillingly, accepted the Emperor's rule.

Kyle's thoughts were elsewhere, however, focused as they were on the back in front of him, and the absolute necessity of staying in step. Especially since graduation from Cliffside involved one final test, a tradition that had emerged with the Empire itself, and had resulted in more than thirty-six deaths.

The test started with a turn to the right, and the long march around the west end of the quad, past the grandstand at the foot of the hospital stairs, past the platform on which General Mohc and a cluster of senior officers stood, past the imposing administration building and the bronze mantigrucs that guarded its doors, and straight for the five-hundred-foot drop from which the academy had taken its unofficial name.

It was a challenge that the cadets had faced countless times during the last four years — and successfully — except for one critical fact. True to tradition, and with safety in mind, they had never faced the abyss itself. During drills, while practicing for this critical moment, a bright yellow line had been used to represent the edge of the dropoff, and like most of his fellow cadets, Kyle could remember what it felt like to stumble, trip, or fall over that symbolic cliff.

The difference was that the consequence for those mistakes consisted of a tongue-lashing followed by fifty pushups, whereas for the *real* thing, a poorly phrased order, a lack of teamwork, or a moment of lost concentration could result in death.

The cadets had spent untold hours arguing over the matter of placement and the relative risks attendant to each position. Each column consisted of four men abreast. Thanks to his medium height, and position in the alphabet, Kyle had been assigned to the sixth rank on the right flank.

While most of his peers felt that this position was not as risky as a slot in the first rank, any placement on the right flank was iffy, as they would skirt the edge of the cliff after the column arrived at the southeast corner of the parade ground and wheeled left.

This was judgment Kyle knew to be true since he had gone to the trouble to research the matter three months before and discovered that of the thirty-six cadets who had fallen to their deaths, fully sixteen had marched on the right flank.

Nathan Donar, who, for reasons transparent to everyone except his toadies, had been given the temporary rank of Cadet Company Commander, marched next to the inside flank and would make the critical call.

Kyle watched the administration building pass through the corner of his eye, quickly followed by the engineering complex, and knew the turn was coming up. Three previous companies had completed the evolution successfully, or so he assumed, but what if Donar made a mistake? What if his voice froze, like what's-his-name — Stor's — had three years previously? The entire front rank had marched off the edge as straight as you please, and the whole bunch of them would have followed if Stor hadn't croaked the word "halt," and reformed the company. The fact that he subsequently took the plunge solo was regarded as unfortunate but fitting. It was held up as an illustration of courage, obedience, and responsibility.

Was it all those things? Or was it just plain stupidity? Kyle had never been able to make up his mind.

Kyle, who thought he had mastered his fear on the asteroid, felt liquid lead trickle into the pit of his stomach and swallowed the lump in his throat.

Donar, conscious of the fact that his mother and father were watching from the grandstand, and that he had an almost overwhelming urge to pee, did his best to penetrate the glare. The trick was to issue the order at exactly the right moment so that the column wheeled, the right flank skimmed the edge of the abyss, and the crowd, their eyes glued to the video provided by hovering camera droids, received the expected thrill.

To aid in the task, and thereby ensure his success, Donar had taken the rather sensible precaution of placing a small self-adhesive disk at the precise point where the turn should begin. This was not in keeping with the Academy's traditions, perhaps. But it was consistent with his father's oft-repeated advice, "Only suckers take chances." Words to live by. The only trouble was that he couldn't see the marker. Was it there? And hidden by the glare? Or had some well-intentioned maintenance droid removed it during the night?

There was no way to know, which meant the Cadet Commander had to do it the hard way. He gulped, forced himself to wait for what he judged to be the last possible moment, and gave the order. "Company! Left turn, march!"

Kyle heard the order, felt the men on his left go into the turn, and took slightly longer steps. The abyss beckoned, came closer, then stabilized. He sensed that a third of his foot was over the edge each time it hit the pavement. Finally, after what seemed like an eternity, the next

order came. "Company! Left turn, march!"

Nothing had ever felt so good as the moment when the company wheeled left and started down the quad's north side. By the time they had completed their circuit and taken up their position in front of the VIP platform, the rest of the cadets had "walked the edge" without casualties.

The fear associated with the abyss quickly turned to boredom as the Commandant introduced the first in a long list of guest speakers, the last of whom was General Mohc. He had a bulldog face, barrel chest, and relatively short frame. He at least was a *real* soldier and worthy of their attention. His speech was short and to the point.

"The Emperor spent more than a half-million credits to feed, house, and educate each one of you over the past four years. Not because he thought it would be the nice thing to do or because he likes military parades, but because he wants you to *defend* the Empire. An Empire which has been attacked from within.

"That's your job. To find the rot, cut it out, and restore order. Not the chaos that flows from a thousand voices demanding a thousand different things, but the consistency that flows from a single, well-conceived plan. The best plan. The right plan. The Emperor's plan. Thank you. And congratulations on your accomplishment."

The next part of the ceremony was extremely important to some of the cadets — those in the top ten percent of the class — and less so to everyone else. In spite of the fact that Kyle had worked hard to make the Commandant's honor roll, he felt ambivalent about being recognized for it. It was as if the mission, and the killing that had been part of it, made everything else seem meaningless.

The Commandant read a list of names and accomplishments over the PA system, while General Mohc, together with a man in a black robe, made their way through the ranks. Though he was not permitted to turn his head from the eyes-forward position, Kyle had excellent peripheral vision, and used it to monitor their progress.

Mohc looked like what he was, an officer who followed orders, no matter how unpleasant they might be. No, it was the other man who held Kyle's eye, who sent a chill down his spine. Why? What was it about the figure in black that he found so frightening? He wasn't sure. The cadet, already at attention, stiffened even more as the men approached. Kyle heard his name boom over the public address system, accepted the honor baton that Mohc handed him, and was surprised to hear his name for a second time.

"And, in recognition for his valor, and bravery in the face of the enemy, the Emperor hereby presents Second Lieutenant Kyle Katarn with the Medal of Valor, as well as the Empire's heartfelt gratitude."

In spite of the noonday sun, Kyle felt the air grow chilly as the other man stepped forward. A hood hung in folds around the hard angles of his face. A narrow strip of black leather obscured the place where his eyes should have been. A tracery of black tattoos swirled away from the corners of his downturned mouth. His voice was as soft as the flutter of bird's wings, yet loud enough to be heard.

"My name is Jerec. Greetings, Kyle Katarn. You have accomplished a great deal for one so young. Recognition is sweet, is it not? However, remember that recognition is a gift given by those who *have* power to those who don't. This is but the first step. Climb the ladder swiftly, join those who *possess* power, and claim what is yours. I will be waiting."

Hands touched his chest, the medal clicked against the magnetic bar sewn into the front of his uniform, and Kyle staggered as power surged through his nervous system. Not from Jerec, but from some place deep within, as if it had been hidden there all along.

For one brief moment Kyle "saw" the entire parade ground as if from above, including the Emperor's statue, the ranks of cadets, a wind-driven food wrapper, and a column of insects foraging for food.

Kyle "heard" the PA, the beating of his own heart, and a tiny almost infinitesimal "click" as the second hand on General Mohc's analog-style chrono advanced to the next position. Kyle "felt" the power of Jerec's mind, understood the extent of his all-consuming hunger, and knew nothing would be allowed to stand between this man and what he wanted. Then Jerec stepped back, the connection snapped, and Kyle was left swaying as if in the wind, his nerves crackling as the final ergs of energy discharged through them.

The rest of the ceremony passed in a haze as Kyle tried to understand what had happened. Why would Jerec say the things he had? Were the words meant to be polite? Or was the invitation genuine? Did it mean what he thought it might? That he could rise to a position similar to Jerec's? And would he want such a thing even if it were possible?

The ceremony ended as it always had, with three cheers for the Emperor, caps tossed into the air, and mass pandemonium as the class was dismissed. Meck Odom appeared out of nowhere, grabbed Kyle around the waist, and lifted him off the ground. Other cadets, eager to see and touch his medal, crowded around. Then, their curiosity satisfied, they headed for the stands where friends and family waited, or back to the dorms, where, assuming they'd been invited, they would prepare for the usual rounds of dinners, dances, and parties. Kyle, like the rest of the rimmers in the class, had been snubbed.

Odom, sensitive to his friend's predicament, threw an arm over his shoulders. "Time to go, blope face, assuming you're willing to consort with peasants, what with your medal and all. Who's the guy in black anyway? A snappy dresser he ain't."

Kyle had to laugh in spite of himself. "Beats me — called himself Jerec for whatever that's worth. Some kind of government official or something."

Odom shrugged. "Whatever. My parents have invited you to dinner. Something about meeting a hero. As though my assault on a deserted weapons factory had no value whatsoever. The nerve of these people!"

Kyle dragged his friend to a halt. "Cut the phobium, Meck. Your parents don't want me. They want *you*. As well they should. I'll take a rain check."

Odom had a square face, dark, nearly black skin, and a perpetual grin. "Negatory on that, O decorated one. Are you coming peaceably? Or shall I drag you?"

Kyle looked, saw the determination in his friend's eyes, and smiled. "Will your sister be there?"

Odom laughed. "Be careful what you ask for, Katarn — you might just get it!"

The evening went well. Unlike so many of the Empire's wealthier families, the Odoms had no ties to the Emperor, and were genuinely nice. Meck's mother ran a small but successful import-export business, and his father was a celebrated architect. They, and their stunning daughter, were splendid hosts and the evening passed with surprising speed.

Finally, so full of good food that Kyle thought he might burst, the cadets returned to the dorm. What with the lifting of their curfew, and the MPs ignoring anything short of total mayhem, there were the predictable number of drunks both pleasant and less so.

The young men dodged the worst of the crazies and made it to their room without major mishap. Kyle had rid himself of his mess jacket, and removed most of his shirt studs, when he noticed that a message icon had appeared in the upper left-hand corner of his computer screen. It blinked with annoying regularity. He almost delayed reading it till morning, certain that it was one of the "Dear Cadet" bulletins that the Commandant loved to issue, but noticed Meck's screen was blank.

Curious, Kyle dropped into his chair, entered his access code, and waited for the message to appear. The words "Receipt Sent" appeared first, followed by the message itself.

"The Emperor regrets to inform you that your father, Morgan Katarn, was killed during a Rebel raid. No further information is available at this time. If you wish to speak with a therapist one will be made available upon request. To apply for compassionate leave select 'Cadet Initiated Administrative Requests' from the main menu and press 'enter.' Choose 'Compassionate Leave,' provide the appropriate information, and attach this message."

Kyle read the words three times before they acquired meaning. Then, sure that the whole thing was part of a cruel hoax perpetrated by one or more of his classmates, he looked for the authentication code that should appear across the bottom of the screen. Tears sprang to his eyes when he saw it. Morgan Katarn, his father, mentor, and best friend, was dead. Killed by the Rebels. Why? Why would they want to kill Morgan Katarn? Especially in light of the fact that his father was sympathetic to the Rebel cause, *too* sympathetic in Kyle's opinion, and had only reluctantly approved his application to the Academy. It didn't make sense. But nothing about war did, including the fact that he had survived while the rest of his team were killed.

Kyle remembered the Comm Center, the Rebels standing with their hands in the air, and knew he had committed a grievous error. Hong had been right. He should have given the order, should have killed every single one of them, should have left a room full of bodies. For the team, for his father, for himself.

Kyle stood, left a note on Meck's nightstand, and headed for the Office of Cadet Affairs. He'd be there when it opened. Maybe they'd have more information, maybe they'd make sense of it, or maybe it was a horrible misunderstanding. Yes, an error that could and would be resolved.

It was cold on the grinder. Moonlight caressed Palpatine's statue and threw darkness across the quad. Kyle, his thoughts as black as space itself, followed.

CHAPTER 4

The *Star of Empire* was more than two kilometers long and equipped to carry five thousand passengers in addition to her considerable crew. The sole property of Haj Shipping Lines, she, like the rest of the company's ships, was a durasteel testament to the family's ability to court favor with the Emperor, while simultaneously maintaining a positive relationship with the burgeoning Alliance. "Let others play at politics — we're in the shipping business," old man Haj liked to say, and, thanks to their cheerful neutrality, the clan prospered as a result.

All of which had nothing to do with Kyle, but everything to do with the *Star*'s diverse passenger list. After hitching a ride on a military transport, Kyle made his way from the Academy on Carida to the orbital transfer station off Dorlon II, where he and a variety of other sentients boarded a well-appointed shuttle.

Now, as Kyle sipped a complimentary glass of wine and watched the *Star* fill the viewport, he found himself shoulder to tentacle with a Twi'lek merchant, a Mon Calamari engineer, a pair of Klatooinian technicians, a Rodian bounty hunter, a Gran of indeterminate profession, and some other species of which he was none too certain. They, plus a variety of specially adapted humanoids, all manner of relatives, bonds beings, and droids made for a cosmopolitan crowd. Quite a change after four years on Carida where nonhumans were rarely seen, much less encountered.

The liner sparkled with decorative lights, her enormous hangar bay yawned to accept them, and the shuttle seemed to drift forward. Kyle admired the precision with which the retros were fired and wondered if he could do as well. He doubted that he could. Practice makes perfect, and he, like all the rest of the Academy's engineering students, had less flight time than he would've liked.

Space-suited crew waited to receive them, droids criss-crossed the deck on various errands, and smaller ships, many of which were the personal property of wealthy passengers, squatted in orderly rows. It was an impressive sight, considerably different from the Carida-bound freighter he had ridden four years before.

It took half an hour to close and pressurize the bay and disembark the shuttle's passengers. Those who could afford first-class accommodations were greeted by members of the *Star*'s eternally solicitous crew and escorted to their various staterooms. Sentients only slightly less fortunate were met by one of the ship's identical purser droids and shown to their smaller but still respectable cabins.

Thanks to the generosity and political savvy of the Haj family, Kyle and a handful of other military personnel were entitled to reduced fares, a thoughtful gesture which pleased the Empire's senior officers. They carried their own luggage as they were herded through a maze of halls, corridors, and tubeways until they arrived on the euphemistically named Starlight Deck, where none of the accommodations had a viewport and the drive chambers were only a bulkhead away.

Kyle had a cubicle-like cabin all to himself, however, which seemed palatial when compared to four years in a shared room. It took less than an hour to take a shower, unpack his gear, and check the terminal. He scanned the ship's layout and settled on the Observation Deck as the most logical destination for someone as poor as he. Unlike many of the restaurants and clubs, it was free, and according to the continually refreshed text, an excellent spot from which to get another look at Dorlon II.

He left the cubicle, checked to make sure the door was locked, and bumped into a Navy rating. They exchanged salutes, nodded to each other, and went their separate ways. Officers didn't fraternize with enlisted people — not openly anyway — and both knew the rules.

It took a while to make his way from the Starlight Deck to the Observation Deck via narrow passageways, crowded lifts, and moving sidewalks. Kyle didn't mind, though, since sentient watching was one of his favorite hobbies, and there were plenty to watch — especially the girls. Having just spent four years in a mostly male environment, Kyle was fascinated by them. So much so that he forgot himself for a moment and didn't realize how obvious he was until the twins he was ogling pointed in his direction, giggled, and said something to their mother. She aimed a frown at the officer, he tripped over his feet, and the girls laughed.

Kyle's face was bright red as they all entered the observation salon.

Thanks to the fact that the area was packed with standing, sitting, reclining, and even squatting sentients, it was easy to get lost in the crowd.

Though different species exhibited a wide variety of behaviors, abilities, and preferences, Kyle had observed that almost all of those equipped with even the most rudimentary organs of sight enjoyed gazing at planets. It didn't matter which planets since, like rocks on a beach, each had its own special kind of beauty.

In fact, there was something about the experience of looking at something so huge, so majestic, that transcended the barriers of species and bound the viewers together. This was such a moment, and while some were engaged in quiet conversation, the vast majority were silent, their attention focused on what lay beyond the transparisteel bubble.

Kyle saw a vast sphere, its surface blackened where volcanoes had spewed ash and lava, gradually giving way to tans, yellows, and a dusting of what looked like powdered sugar where sulfur compounds dominated the soil.

Others, those who were limited to the gray scale, or beings who had the capacity to detect infrared emanations, saw different but no less impressive sights, each according to his, her, or its abilities.

Kyle winced as an all-too-familiar voice sounded from behind him. "Rimmer? Didn't know you were booked aboard the *Star* — could have offered you a lift. Family yacht you know — safely stashed below."

Kyle forced a smile as he turned. "Nathan. What a pleasant surprise. How's the hangover?"

Donar, who had consumed too much wine on graduation night and had thrown up all over the inside of a friend's ground car, looked left and right. His drinking was a sore subject where his mother was concerned, and he didn't want another lecture. "Long gone, old rimmer, long gone. Come now, enough rubbernecking, it's time to meet my parents. In fact, how 'bout lunch? The old man's rather fond of a good feed and we can latch on."

With the single exception of Meck Odom and his family, it was the first time that Kyle had received such an invitation, and in spite of the fact that he knew the gap between rimmer and the Empire's inner circle to be all but unbridgeable, he couldn't help feeling complimented. Besides, what with Nathan dragging him through the crowd, and his parents already in sight, there was no way to refuse. Nasal though it was, Nathan's voice was loud, and cut through the noise. "Mother . . . Father . . . look who I ran into? I'd like you to meet Kyle Katarn — you know, the cadet who won the medal."

Although the honorable Madame Donar looked pleasant if somewhat emaciated, Nathan's father, Dol Donar II, Governor of Derra IV, was something else again. He was an imposing man, as portly as his wife was thin, with eyes like twin turbolasers, and three chins. His clothing, which shimmered with reflected light, hung in great folds, as if to conceal his weight. He regarded Kyle with a look akin to an entomologist examining a brand-new specimen. The words, as nasal as his son's, came like jabs. "Decorated, you say? When? Why?"

Nathan, who was used to his father's style, was quick to explain. "During the graduation ceremony — for valor on a Rebel-held asteroid."

The Governor extended a beefy hand. Kyle noticed that he wore a pinkie ring set with what must have been a five-karat Rol Stone. It sparkled with light. "Of course. Silly of me to forget! Congratulations, son. A medal of valor is something to be proud of."

"As was your son's leadership during the graduation ceremony," Kyle replied tactfully. "I wouldn't be here if it weren't for his judgment."

The older man smiled and put an arm around Nathan's shoulders. "It was something to see, I can tell you that! You lads did a fine job. Scared the heck out of his mother, though."

Nathan, who lived to earn his father's respect, turned pink with pleasure and chattered nonstop through the subsequent lunch. The Nebula Room was one of the most expensive restaurants onboard. Kyle, who could have subsisted for a week on the food Governor Donar consumed during that single meal, settled for a green salad, a freshly baked scone, a serving of runyip stew, and then, because he couldn't resist, a bowl of candied insects. The dish was a favorite among the Kubaz, and the dessert chef brought it to the table himself. Kyle had just consumed the last of the sweet-and-sour morsels when Governor Donar turned his way. "So, tell us about your family, son, what line of business are they in?"

Nathan frowned and looked genuinely sorry as Kyle forced himself to look the older man in the eye. "My father was a craftsman — the Rebels murdered him."

The statement was a clear admission of social inferiority, but, rather than showing disdain as Kyle had feared, the Governor was genuinely outraged. "Rebels, you say? Blast their miserable hides! A pox on every one of them!"

Madame Donar, who was well aware of the fact that the sentients seated around them might be Rebels, or Rebel sympathizers, placed a hand on her husband's arm. "Your voice carries, Dol. Remember where we are."

"I don't care where we are!" Donar declared loudly, ignoring those who turned to stare. "I've said it before, and I'll say it again: The only *good* Rebel is a *dead* Rebel! Mark my words, son, the Emperor has a thing or two in store for the so-called Alliance, and your father *will* be revenged."

The way the man said it, the certainty of his expression, all led Kyle to believe that something real lay behind the words. Whatever it was must be awesome indeed if the Empire was to suppress the kind of fanaticism he'd encountered on Asteroid AX-456. He was about to say as much when a well-dressed man approached the table. He bowed to Madame Donar and turned to her husband.

"Madame Donar. Governor. Please allow me to introduce myself. The name is Calrissian, Lando Calrissian, and I hear that you enjoy the occasional game of sabacc."

Madame Donar, whose lunch had consisted of little more than some leaves with berries on them, frowned and tried to establish eye contact with the Governor. It was too late, however, since a gleam had entered his eyes and eagerness colored his voice. "Sabacc, you say? Lando Calrissian? It's a pleasure to meet you, citizen Calrissian. Please allow me to introduce my wife Rissa, my son Nathan, and his friend Kyle Katarn. I'd be glad to join you and your friends, assuming it's a friendly game, consistent with my somewhat limited skills."

Calrissian bowed from the waist. "I expect the game to be extremely friendly. And I sense you are far too modest regarding your skills. The Corellia room, then? About two?"

"The Corellia room at two."

Calrissian nodded to each person seated at the table and walked away.

—+— ⅜✧⅜ —+—

Nathan and his father departed for the Corellia room immediately after lunch, while Madame Donar, who had developed a headache, retired to the family's suite. Kyle thanked them for lunch, promised to visit the game, and went for a walk.

Now, away from the nearly fanatical Imperialism of Carida, and outside the protective bubble that surrounded the Donar family, Kyle began to pick up on the hatred that seethed just below the Empire's surface. There were long hard looks, shoulders that seemed to intentionally bump into his, and comments, some loud enough to hear.

"Imperial scum!"

"Stormtrooper!"

"Slimeball."

The comments made him embarrassed, angry, and confused all at the same time. Didn't they understand? Didn't they know what the Rebels had done? Surely they couldn't be so stupid. But apparently they were, as occasional bits of graffiti confirmed.

Discouraged, and more than a little depressed, Kyle headed for one place where he felt sure he'd be accepted — the Corellia room. Like all the rest of the world-class public rooms, the Corellia had been decorated with its namesake in mind.

Rather than the transparisteel viewport one might have expected, the outer bulkhead featured a vid screen designed to look like a viewport. The image projected there was so real, so convincing, that if Kyle hadn't known better, he would have sworn the ship was orbiting Corellia herself. That, plus cases filled with Corellian artifacts, and walls hung with Corellian art, gave the space its unique look and feel.

The game was well under way by the time Kyle arrived. It had attracted a good many onlookers. Nathan bade him welcome, as did the Governor, but both were preoccupied. There were twenty-five or thirty beings present, but only four were seated at the game table.

Their cards, dealt by one of the ship's game droids, bore electronically generated images. There were four suits — staves, flasks, sabres, and coins. Each could be scrambled through the use of a button located at the lower left-hand corner of the card. And there were various sets of rules, including the Empress Teta Preferred system, Cloud City Casino, Corellian Gambit, and at least one more that Kyle couldn't remember. The simple truth was that he'd never enjoyed games much. He was, he had to admit, a sore loser.

Kyle looked up from the table, and caught a glimpse of a face that looked familiar. Or did it? The face belonged to a girl, and much as he might want to, Kyle didn't know any girls. He stared, but she disappeared behind a pair of head-tailed Twi'leks on the far side of the table. Kyle moved to the left, trying to get a better look at her, and accidentally bumped into a Rodian bounty hunter. It was hard to say which was worse, the alien's body odor, or the cheap cologne he used to conceal it.

Suddenly, like clouds parting to admit a ray of sunlight, two of the onlookers moved apart. The girl looked his way, their eyes met, and they recognized each other. It was her! The girl from the asteroid!

Kyle saw her eyes widen in surprise, saw an emotion he couldn't quite identify cross her face, and watched her turn away. Without thinking, Kyle followed her as she moved quickly through the crowd.

He told himself that it was her status as a Rebel — that he was doing his duty — but he knew it was something more. He wanted to hurt her, to punish her for everything the Rebels had done. But he wanted to talk with her, too. She had been there on the asteroid, and she might be the only person who could understand the way he felt.

Kyle rounded the table, sidestepped the droid that never seemed to stray very far from Calrissian's side, and lunged for the door. The Rodian bounty hunter, his large purple eyes empty of all expression,

watched him go. Outside, Kyle saw little more than a flash of blue as the girl merged onto a moving walkway.

Running to catch up, Kyle dodged, passed, and brushed any number of sentients, murmured "Excuse me" over and over again, kept both eyes on his quarry. Once on the walkway, he moved to the outside lane, passed a businesswoman and her secretarial droid, and broke into a fast walk.

The girl had a significant lead on him by then. She looked back over her shoulder, confirmed that he was there, and walked even faster. Seeing that, Kyle redoubled his efforts, broke into a jog. He failed to notice the tall, nearly cadaverous man who touched the plug in his right ear, murmured "Waller here — he's on the way," into a comlink, and ambled along behind.

The walkway ended, the girl paused long enough for Kyle to get a fix on her, then headed for a lift tube. The young officer pushed his way through the crowd, apologized right and left, and arrived in front of the lift just as it closed.

Kyle pounded on the metal in frustration, ignored a droid's offer of help, and watched the indicator light. There were two levels below the one he was on, but the second was off limits to passengers, which told him what he needed to know.

The ladderway, which was intended for emergencies and only rarely used, ran parallel to the tube. Kyle touched the panel next to the access door, waited for it to slide out of the way, and stepped inside. The ladder was designed to accommodate both gravity and null gravity conditions. He clamped his feet against the outside rails and used his hands as brakes. The ship's artificial gravity handled the rest.

The descent lasted five seconds. His boots hit the next platform at the same moment that someone threw a choke hold around his neck. Kyle pried at the arm but found it was useless. He might as well have been trying to bend a durasteel bar. The words warmed the right side of his face. "So what's the hurry, bucko? What if you fell and broke your neck? What would the Emperor do then?"

Kyle tried to say something, tried to respond, but could only make a gargling sound. Another voice intervened. It was distinctly feminine. "That's enough, Rosco. The passageway is clear. Bring him out."

As if by magic, the choke hold metamorphosed into a wrist-lock. Rosco applied some leverage, and Kyle winced and turned toward the hatch. The girl waited to make sure the officer was still under control, nodded approvingly, and stepped into the passageway. Kyle, with some encouragement from Rosco, followed.

Rosco was built like a barrel. He had a blond crew cut, fist-flattened nose, and tiny blue eyes. They sparkled knowingly. "Life sucks, don't it? 'Specially if you're a no-good, slime-sucking Imperial parasite."

Kyle, who knew he was being baited, remained silent. His chance would come, or so his unarmed-combat instructor had promised, and patience was the key.

A tall thin man appeared as if out of nowhere and fell in behind them. Kyle realized that while his capture hadn't been planned in advance, it had been coordinated on the fly, and expertly at that. Say what you might about the Rebs, they were competent.

The girl stopped in front of a hatch, entered a series of numbers into the key pad, and waited for the door to open. Kyle caught a glimpse of storeroom shelves, realized his captors had support from at least one member of the ship's crew, and wondered if there were other privileges as well.

The girl stepped aside and Kyle was shoved through the opening. The young officer stumbled, fell, and hit the deck face down. He did a pushup, brought his knees under his torso, and launched a backward kick. His left foot missed but his right made contact with Rosco's knee. Kyle fell, rolled, and scrambled to his feet.

Most people would have screamed, grabbed the place where it hurt, and collapsed to the floor. The Rebel wasn't most people. He gave a grunt of surprise, frowned, and was about to retaliate when the girl spoke. "Hold it right there. You asked for that one, Rosco — and learned something in the bargain. The Lieutenant may not *look* like much, but he took AX-456."

"All the more reason to kill him," Rosco growled. "I had friends on 456."

"And I was *stationed* there," the girl replied steadily, her eyes locked with Kyle's. "He could have killed us, *should* have killed us. But he didn't. That took guts."

Kyle searched her face for the hate, for the evil that had killed his father, and couldn't find it. What he saw were the same calm eyes that had connected with his on the asteroid, the same unwavering determination, and yes, the thing he had hoped for but least expected to see: understanding. She knew the taste of fear, the weight of command, and the horror of defeat. The thin man cleared his throat. "So? Where does that leave us?"

The girl raised an eyebrow. "What's it going to be, Imperial? You gave me my life. I'll give you yours."

The answer came so easily that Kyle felt a sense of guilt. "I'll take it."

The girl nodded, glanced at the thin man's weapon, and said, "Stow the hardware."

The blaster stayed where it was. "Why should we trust him? The fact that he isn't entirely heartless doesn't qualify him as an ally."

The girl stepped forward and held out her hand. It felt cool and dry. "I'm Jan Ors — and you are?"

"Kyle Katarn."

"Glad to meet you, Kyle. Do I have your word? No funny business so long as we're aboard this ship?"

Kyle nodded soberly. "You have my word."

Rosco gave a grunt of disgust. "And what would that be worth? A Hutt's breakfast?"

Ors ignored him. "All right then, we go our way, and you go yours. Remember, though — my debt's been paid. And all bets are off next time we meet."

Kyle felt a sudden sense of desperation. The girl had told him good-bye. There would be no next time. The thin man had backed into the passageway and Ors would follow. "Wait — I want to talk to you — to learn more about what happened."

The words sounded lame, terribly lame, but caused the girl to pause. Her eyes softened slightly. "Talk? And that's all? You won't attempt to turn me in, or something stupid like that?"

Kyle shook his head. "No. I promise."

"All right," the girl agreed. "We'll talk. But we'll do it in public, where everyone can see. The library. One hour from now."

Kyle nodded. "The library. I'll see you there."

Jan Ors smiled and disappeared.

* ⚑ *

The ship's library, which was actually a great deal more than that, included millions of books in thousands of languages, all stored electronically. There were interactive virtual-reality games, tutorials, and much, much more. Because of the fact that most of the materials could be accessed remotely, or copied into data pads, the facility occupied relatively little space.

Perhaps it was the library's size, or the time of day, but the first thing Kyle noticed was that it was relatively empty. Oh, there were people all right, but no more than a dozen or so, most of whom were lost in whatever text or scenario their scanners were playing, or in one case — a Rodian — seemingly asleep in a cubicle.

Given the fact that Kyle was early, he didn't expect to see Jan, and was surprised when he did. The raised area, intended for readings, was small but adequate for a single performer. Kyle looked around, found no one to take his cues from, and took one of five empty seats.

In spite of the fact that he couldn't see whatever it was that she saw, or hear the music that so clearly moved her, he knew pure, unalloyed talent when he saw it. More than that — Kyle knew he was looking at an important aspect of who Jan Ors was.

Jan watched the other dancers out of the corner of her eye, waited for the music that would bring them around, matched their jeté, turned to a pirouette, and held an arabesque. It collapsed for the lack of pointe shoes and the practice necessary to sustain it, but applause thundered nonetheless, and flowers landed around her feet.

The whole thing looked so real, and sounded so real, that for one fleeting second Jan imagined it *was* real and took a bow. Then, as the sound died away, and the video started to fade, she lifted the visor. She was shocked to see him sitting there, to hear the sound of his clapping, and heard herself lash out. "You don't have anything better to do than make fun of me?"

Kyle looked hurt. "You have it wrong. You were wonderful. Where did you learn to dance like that?"

Somewhat mollified, and secretly pleased, Jan retrieved her blue coverall and stepped into the lower half. "When I was a little girl. My mother was the choreographer for Alderaan's premier ballet company. And I was raised between rehearsals."

"And your father?"

Jan's head was tilted forward. She regarded him from under raised eyebrows. "Nosy, aren't you? My father was — and as far as I know still is — a first class aerospace engineer. Hand me those boots."

Kyle looked around, saw a pair of well-scuffed boots, and bent to retrieve them. "Really? Does that mean you can repair drives as well as you dance?"

"Yes," Jan said matter-of-factly, "it does. How 'bout you, sparky? Got any talents other than the ones you demonstrated on that asteroid?"

Kyle frowned. "I went to the Academy to get an education. I'm more engineer than soldier."

"Yeah, and I'm a dancer," Jan said skeptically. "Come on. I'm thirsty."

The cafeteria catered to the less prosperous members of the passenger list and was half full. They waited through the line, made inconsequential small talk, and obtained their drinks. Kyle offered to pay and Jan allowed him to do so. It seemed natural to seek out the most distant and therefore private part of the room. They sat down, sipped their drinks, and regarded each other across the table. "So,"

Jan offered noncommittally. "You wanted to talk."

Kyle shrugged. "Yeah . . . You probably won't believe me, but most of the troopers who died on that asteroid were good men."

Jan was silent for a moment. When she spoke, her voice was soft but determined. "A lot of good people died that day, Kyle. Some were on my side — some were on yours. That's how war is. You chose to be a soldier. What did you expect?"

Kyle felt an unexpected surge of anger. "Yeah? Well, what about my father? He was a craftsman, not a soldier, and the Rebs killed him anyway. Explain that."

Given his tone, and the partisan nature of the subject, Kyle half expected her to leave the table. To his surprise, and subsequent relief, she made no such move. In fact, her expression could better be described as one of surprise. "What planet?"

Kyle was taken aback. "A moon called Sulon. It orbits Sullust."

She nodded. "I'm aware of it. Your father's name?"

"Same as mine. Katarn. Morgan Katarn."

"And where did you get the idea that your father died at the hands of the Alliance?"

Kyle shrugged. "The Commandant sent me a message."

Jan shook her head in apparent amazement. "My mother says the Force moves in mysterious ways — and I never cease to be amazed at how right she is. Come on — I want you to meet someone."

——◄══❖══►——

Knowing that open contact with members of the Rebel Alliance could easily bring him to the attention of the Emperor's spies, Kyle made his way to Jan's cabin on his own. He touched the sensor pad. A tone sounded within and the hatch whirred open.

Whether due to luck, the connivance of a Rebel sympathizer, or a more generous budget than Kyle would have supposed, Jan's cabin was slightly larger than his. However, the fact that she shared the space with a chrome-plated translator droid more than compensated for that particular advantage. The machine came to life as Jan spoke its name. "A-Cee. I want to introduce someone."

The droid's head came up and servos whirred as he looked in Kyle's direction. What happened next took both humans by surprise. A-Cee stiffened, backed even further into the corner, and spoke in a hard unyielding voice: "I am a bomb. Unauthorized access, manipulation, or interference with me or my programming, data storage modules, or other systems will result in the detonation of four point two kilos of plitex nine

I am a bomb

Unauthorized Access

manipulation or

interference

with

me

or my program

will result in

the detonation

42 kilos of plitex 9

5 ... 4 ... 3 ... 2 ...

explosive. I have identified a class three threat, and, in accordance with my programming, am taking appropriate action. Detonation sequence activated. Countdown initiated. Ten — nine — eight . . . "

Kyle took a step towards the hatch and looked at Jan. She ran the words together in her eagerness to get them out. "Override code alpha, bravo, zeta, one-niner-six. Execute."

A-Cee paused, broke the countdown sequence, and seemed to relax. "Override authenticated. Detonation sequence terminated."

Jan looked at Kyle and grinned weakly. "Sorry about that. It was the uniform, combined with the fact that he's something of an orphan. The reason will become apparent in a moment. First, answer a question. When they sent your team to 456, did they say why?"

Kyle frowned. "No, not exactly. They said the objective was to take a communications relay station — no more than that."

Jan nodded. "Well, the information they gave you was accurate so far as it went, but there's more. The truth about the Emperor and his many atrocities is one of the most potent weapons the Alliance has. Once aware of it, neutral parties become more sympathetic, new alliances are formed, and support is solidified. The vast distances that separate the Empire's planets make that difficult, however."

Kyle started to object but Jan raised her hand. "Hear me out — see with your own eyes — then say what you will.

"The Alliance has reporters, brave men and women who roam from planet to planet, often within Imperial-controlled space, collecting stories for dissemination to those willing to see, hear, and understand. Many of these correspondents have companions like A-Cee here, who are equipped to capture, store, and edit whatever they witness. Once the stories have been prepared, they are distributed throughout the Empire via communications relay stations like the one on Asteroid 456."

Kyle, who was none too pleased by all the anti-Imperial propaganda inherent in what she'd said, crossed his arms. "This is all very interesting. But why should I care?"

Jan was silent for a moment, and, for reasons he couldn't understand, looked sorry for him. "Kyle, there's no way in heck that I should show you this, but I'm going to do it anyway. Remember the reporters I mentioned? Well, A-Cee was assigned to a woman named Candice Ondi. She was one of our best correspondents and died covering the story you're about to see. A-Cee — show Lieutenant Katarn the battle for the Sulon G-Tap."

Servos whined as A-Cee stepped to the computer terminal, withdrew a cable from the compartment located on the lower right side of his torso, and made a connection to the input panel. There was a moment of black followed by a holo of a pleasant-looking middle-aged woman. She introduced herself as Candice Ondi and said she was reporting from the site of an impending battle.

Kyle recognized the place immediately. There was no mistaking the canyon and the cavern. Thanks to the urging of his father and other influential members of the community, initial survey work had been under way before he left for the Academy.

Ondi described recent raids by stormtroopers disguised as Rebels, offered some none-too-convincing home video as evidence to support her allegations, and alluded to "confidential sources of information" that had warned of a major assault on the G-Tap.

Then, as the droid-mounted holocam panned across the cavern's interior, Kyle saw a sight that caused his heart to skip a beat. His father, Morgan Katarn, addressing a rag-tag group of teenagers and senior citizens. Kyle knew most of them by their first names. His father — a Rebel leader — the knowledge came as a shock. Ondi's commentary made the scene all the more moving.

"As you can see, when it comes to battling the Empire, both young and old agree. This group, under the command of a local militia leader, will defend a passageway the locals refer to as the 'back door.'"

Kyle, who had vivid memories of playing hide-and-seek through the passageway in question, felt a lump form in his throat. He came to his feet. The story wasn't true, it couldn't be! But even the possibility made his palms sweat. The rest was worse.

Ondi and her faithful droid were there when Major Noda and his carefully disguised stormtroopers pushed their way up the river. Kyle, who had been more than a little cynical about the veracity of the report, experienced a sinking feeling as the first AT-ST appeared, only to be destroyed by a Rebel SLM.

Yes, he caught a glimpse of the Rebel designator painted on the machine's flanks, but knew how easily that could be faked. Especially since it was so difficult to envision a scenario in which Rebels had captured the machines and put them to such casual use. More than anything, though, it was the way the attackers moved up river that convinced him of the report's authenticity. Every action they took was right out of the Academy's manuals, and, as his father liked to say, "If it sounds like a bantha, walks like a bantha, and smells like a bantha, chances are it's a bantha."

Then, just as another AT appeared around the bend, and the rate of incoming fire increased, Ondi turned to the camera. She was about to say something, about to comment on the action, when a look of surprise came over her face. She'd been hit, and the footage as A-Cee ran to catch her was more eloquent than words. She tried to say something as she lay cradled in the droid's arms, frowned when the words refused to come, and lost all expression.

The holo faded to black and silence settled over the cabin. When Kyle spoke the words came as a croak. "I'm sorry about Ondi. Do you have any idea what happened to my father?"

He saw something unreadable in Jan's eyes. Pity? Compassion? Sorrow? He couldn't tell. Her voice was gentle. "A-Cee took some additional video — but I'm not sure that I should show it."

"Show me what you have," Kyle said grimly. "I want to know how my father died."

The droid looked at Jan inquiringly and she nodded her head. The screen came to life and Kyle found himself peeking out through a gap where a tarp had come loose and flapped in the breeze. Trees whipped by and beyond them Kyle saw the warehouses that lined the western perimeter of Sulon's spaceport and the northern outskirts of Baron's Hed. A checkpoint manned by men in glossy white armor appeared. There was a moment of darkness as A-Cee pulled back, followed by the sound of gears, and a brief glimpse of run-down buildings as the vehicle moved forward.

Then, safely through the checkpoint, A-Cee returned to work. The road paralleled the spaceport. Kyle saw a graffiti-defaced wall appear, noticed the strange-looking bumps that lined the top, and wondered why the birds liked them so much. There were hundreds, maybe thousands of flitting wings, bursting into flight at the slightest hint of danger, only to settle again.

Then, as the road moved up against the wall, and the truck started to slow, Kyle realized the bumps were human heads. He was still absorbing that, still struggling to deal with it, when the truck ground to a halt. Kyle saw his father's face, felt his lunch rise, and forced it back down.

There was more, but Jan signaled A-Cee to stop and the droid obeyed. Jan, unsure of what to do or say, watched Kyle's face. She saw sadness appear there, quickly followed by anger, and hardening resolve. He seemed to age before her eyes, and when he spoke, the words came as if from another man. "Thank you. The truth can hurt. But lies are worse."

Then, in a gesture that Jan would never forget, the officer ripped the bar that symbolized his Medal of Valor from the front of his uniform and threw it in the recycling bin. The Empire didn't know it, but a Rebel had been born.

CHAPTER 5

Jan entered the lock with a Mon Calamari pilot and a pair of maintenance droids. None felt the need to communicate, and they passed the time by watching the status board. The wait was relatively short, thanks to the fact that the hangar deck was pressurized.

A tone warbled its way from sub- to ultrasonic, an indicator light glowed green, and for those equipped to see it, an infrared blob appeared as well.

The hatch opened and everyone stepped out. In spite of the fact that Jan enjoyed the often awe-inspiring views available from the *Star*'s many observation ports, the hangar deck was her favorite part of the ship. Not the hangar bay itself, but the endlessly fascinating ships parked therein.

Most were relatively small and belonged to passengers who preferred the liner's comfort to a long, monotonous trip aboard their own ships. That being the case, the Rebel agent saw all manner of vessels, including a work-worn lighter, a converted pinnace, numerous shuttles, and a barge equipped for long-distance cruising.

It was a joy to walk among them, to touch atmosphere-scorched metal, inhale the smell of ozone, and exchange greetings with sentients who, like herself, enjoyed the kinesthetic feedback received while turning, pulling, bending, welding, connecting, bolting, and snapping parts into place.

Jan knew that her enjoyment of such things, like her ability to dance, was a gift from her parents. And while others might see them as two separate talents, she knew they stemmed from the same impulse, a need to translate thoughts to motion. All of which had something to do with the fact that the agent had little to no interest in stationary machines.

Jan passed under a blunt-nosed bow, took note of a badly bent landing skid, and stopped in front of the aptly named *Truly Sorry*. Once classified as a speedster, the ship had outlived that description and was anything but fast. Beggars can't be choosers, however, not if they work for the credit-strapped Alliance, and the *Sorry* had been assigned to her. Until this mission was completed, that is. Then Jan would lobby for something better. Assuming the miserable pile of junk didn't kill her in the meantime.

Jan punched a string of numbers into the key pad located next to the belly hatch, winced as the badly worn actuator stuttered, and waited for the ramp to touch the lubricant-stained deck.

Her tools, the best money could buy, were stored in a high-quality self-propelled box located in the ship's tiny cargo compartment. She whistled, waited for the storage unit to trundle down the ramp, and thumbed the print lock. The lid whirred open, a tier of drawers popped free, and a power cable slithered toward an outlet.

The first and potentially most dangerous maintenance problem lay in the ship's hyperspace motivator, which had a tendency to produce false propulsion readings. That was a serious malady in light of the fact that the formula used to calculate hyperspace jumps required precise information regarding the ship's speed.

To access the motivator and run the necessary checks, Jan would have to free a belly plate, disconnect the wiring harness, and remove the lower half of the motivator housing. It was a long and not very stimulating job.

More than two hours passed before Jan backed the last bolt out of the motivator housing and heard it clatter on the deck. The agent realized her mistake the moment the casing dropped into her hands. The *Sorry*'s ancient metal-heavy housing weighed in excess of a hundred kilos. She should have used a hydraulic floor jack or, failing that, summoned a maintenance droid. The unit sagged, she struggled to support it, and wondered what to do.

She could holler for help. But it was unlikely that anyone would hear over the chatter of power tools and the beep, beep, beep of passing auto carts. Or, and this seemed more likely, she could jump out of the way and allow the housing to hit the deck.

Chances were that everything would be fine. But what if the casing developed a hair-thin crack? Or took a dent she couldn't pound out? The odds of finding a replacement aboard the *Star* were not good. All because she hadn't asked for help, a tendency her mother had first noticed when she was four years old.

The voice startled her. "That looks heavy. Can I lend a hand?"

Unable to speak, and shaking from the strain, Jan nodded her head. At least half the weight seemed to disappear as Kyle Katarn added his strength to the effort and they lowered the casing to the floor. "Should have used a floor jack, or called for a maintenance droid," he said maddeningly. "You could have hurt yourself."

Jan bit off the retort that threatened to launch itself from her lips. "Yeah — good thing you stopped by."

Kyle nodded absently. "Nice set of tools you have there. Must have cost a bundle. Need any help?" He looked hopeful and a little bit lost.

Jan wanted to say "No," wanted to chase Kyle away, but took pity on him instead. "Sure. Let's see if the Academy taught you anything useful. I'll work on the wiring harness — you tackle the diagnostics."

Kyle nodded. "Mind if I use your tools?"

"No, but thanks for asking."

The following hour passed in companionable silence. Though busy with her own tasks, Jan watched Kyle out of the corner of her eye. She was impressed by his knowledge and the surety of his hands. He knew his way around a hyperdrive and treated her tools with respect. Finally, after wiping his hands on an oily rag, Kyle delivered his diagnosis. "The sensor package is shot — and the power breaker needs adjusting."

Jan had arrived at the same conclusion. "Good, especially in light of the fact that the sensor package is one of the few things we have a replacement for. Back in a minute."

Jan was halfway to the ramp when Kyle spoke. "Jan . . . "

"Yeah?"

"I want to join. I want to do the kind of work you do."

She looked at him, saw the commitment in his eyes, and nodded. "I don't have the authority to recruit agents, Kyle. But I know the people who do. We're scheduled to part company with the *Star* two days from now, assuming our repairs hold. You're welcome to come along."

Kyle nodded solemnly. "Count me in."

"Good," Jan said. "Help boost that motivator housing into place, and you fly first class."

Kyle laughed.

Neither noticed the tiny caterpillarlike microdroid that crawled along the top surface of a support strut, or heard the high-frequency transmission it sent.

The cabin was almost dark and more than half filled with trophies, including an assassin droid's head, a con woman's four-barreled hold-out blaster, a spy's bionic arm, a bank robber's satchel, and much, much more.

Each trophy was precious to the cabin's sole occupant, and would occupy special niches in the home he would excavate one day. But that was then — and this was now. His name was Slyder, and he listened to the Rebels with the same attention a banker lavishes on her head accountant. Human languages and diction were tricky at times, and mistakes could be fatal. Not that any part of his profession was especially safe.

Like many Rodians, Slyder was a bounty hunter. And a very successful one. No thanks to his tracking skills, which were mediocre at best, or his expertise with weapons, which was average, but because of the way he did his job.

Most of Slyder's peers, Rodians and other species alike, practiced their profession in the same time-honored manner: Wait for someone or something to post a reward, pursue the being in question, and kill or capture the quarry. This was a strategy that Slyder regarded as reactive, dangerous, and work-intensive.

His approach, which was unique to him so far as he knew, was to identify subjects that should have a price on their heads, identify the client willing to pay for his services, and then consummate the deal. By doing so he eliminated most, if not all, of the competition and maintained greater control over the enterprise. The *Star*, and the sentients she carried, made an ideal hunting ground, and saved the time and energy involved in running all over the Empire. Which explained why Slyder had lived in the same cabin for the past three years.

And which also explained his interest in Jan Ors, Kyle Katarn, Rosco Ross, and Ris Waller. The Empire, which maintained a long list of real and fancied enemies, was one of Slyder's best customers, and there was nothing they liked better, or paid more for, than Rebel agents.

Slyder grabbed a tube of pol pollen, popped the cork, and inhaled the substance through his snoutlike nose. The stimulant, which had consumed more and more of his income of late, boosted his ability to reason. Or so it seemed whenever he took it. There were three Rebel agents, each profitable in their own right, plus a droid, which might or might not have value, and a fledgling officer, who for reasons not apparent, was ready to desert. A profitable trip indeed.

Not only that, but an Imperial official happened to be on board, which not only created the perfect market for his goods, but bypassed the need to negotiate with petty officialdom. Slyder found the thought so good, so pleasing, that he rewarded himself with another dose of pollen.

⊷ ⚎⚎ ⊶

The Donar suite was large and spacious. Stasis-fresh flowers, compliments of old man Haj, filled every available vase. A case of wine accompanied by a note from the Bonadan ambassador sat unopened in a corner. Crates of Caridian glassware, secured against an unexpected loss of gravity, sat against the inner bulkhead. Carefully selected pieces of Empire-style furniture sat in front of a large but mostly empty viewport.

All the members of the Donar family, each lost in their own world, were silent except for the occasional cough or rustle of fabric. The Governor had lost far too many credits to Lando Calrissian, and Madame Donar was angry. That being the case, he struggled to find a reason, any reason to avoid her. Especially given the fact that the ring she had given him on their twentieth wedding anniversary was gracing Lando Calrissian's hand rather than his. Had she noticed? And if she hadn't, should he attempt to win the keepsake back? No matter how hard he stared at the computer screen, it was blank.

The Governor looked up as the family protocol droid entered the room. He wore a black cutaway coat and made a noise similar to that of a man clearing his throat. Donar was thankful for the diversion. "Yes? What is it?"

"A visitor, sir . . . His name is Slyder — he regrets the intrusion — but insists on seeing you."

Madame Donar sat in a corner, pretending to work on her embroidery, while Nathan Donar, one leg hanging over the arm of his chair, looked up from a sports printout.

Governor Donar, aware of their interest, waved his approval. "Yes, yes, show the gentleman in."

The protocol droid bowed and backed away. Slyder, who wished the lights were dimmer, entered, searched for the Governor, and found him. He hated the fat human on sight — and wished there was a bounty on his head. "Greetings, Excellency. Stories of your wisdom, generosity, and strength are more numerous than the stars."

The Rodian's naturally foul body odor, overlaid by the scent of his cologne, penetrated every corner of the room. Nathan smirked, his mother covered her nose, and Donar looked annoyed. He made no attempt to rise, nor did he invite the alien to sit.

"May I be of assistance, citizen Slyder? A matter of some urgency, I believe?"

Slyder touched hand to forehead in what Donar assumed was a gesture of respect. It conveyed just the opposite. "Your Excellency

79

steals the words straight from my snout. I, like many members of my species, make a living as a bounty hunter. Not from a desire to accumulate credits, but out of our love for the Empire."

"Yes, of course," the Governor said impatiently. "So what are you selling?"

Slyder touched his forehead once again. "Your Excellency cuts to the very heart of the matter. There are at least three Rebel agents aboard this ship, plus a droid who may or may not carry valuable data. And an Imperial officer who seems ready to desert."

The Governor came to his feet. His computer clattered to the floor. "An officer? Rebels? Who? Where?"

Slyder made his way to the entertainment center and held a holocube up to the light. "May I?"

Donar nodded and the cube went in. Light swirled and a series of three-dimensional images appeared. Slyder allowed key scenes to play themselves out and made no attempt to narrate the action. There were snatches of clearly seditious conversation between the woman and her companions, a glimpse of the droid she kept hidden in her cabin, plus two conversations with Katarn. The exchange in the cafeteria seemed innocent enough, but the subsequent encounter was something else again.

Nathan didn't know what to believe. Was Kyle guilty of treasonous conduct? Or the victim of a pretty face? The holo disappeared and Nathan looked at his father. The governor was livid. "Damn their miserable lies! Did you see that? Sending trollops to corrupt our officers! We'll arrest the lot of them and put an end to this outrage!"

Slyder dry-washed his hands, nodded sanctimoniously, and remembered the officer's Medal of Valor. It would look good in his trophy case.

⊷ ⊨◊⊨ ⊶

Kyle stepped out of the fresher, wiped the remaining water from his skin, and started to dress. He had nearly finished when a tone sounded and a message icon appeared. Curious, Kyle touched a key and watched words flood the screen. The send box was blank, but the greeting was a dead giveaway.

"Hey, rimmer — just a word to the wise — stay clear of the girl — and be ready to answer some questions. She's pretty — but not pretty enough to waste a career on." There was no signature — just a blinking cursor.

Nathan's meaning was clear. Governor Donar, or someone close to him, knew about the Rebels.

Kyle felt his stomach muscles tighten as he punched the numbers and waited for Jan to answer. Her voice was sleepy, as if she had just awoken. "Hello?"

"Listen carefully. Someone, my guess is Governor Donar, knows about you and the others. They could arrive at any moment."

Jan was far too professional to waste time on questions. "Roger that. Grab what you can, and meet us on the hangar deck."

Kyle hit the off button, felt guilty about the manner in which he had betrayed Nathan's confidence, and remembered the picture of his father's decapitated head. His mouth made a hard, thin line as he strapped the Imperial-issue side arm around his waist, threw his personal items in a carryall, and left the cabin. His uniforms, with the single exception of the one on his back, remained in the closet.

Jan peeked through the peephole, assured herself that the area in front of the entry was clear, and opened the hatch. A quick check confirmed that the hallway was empty. She turned to the droid. "There isn't much time, A-Cee. Let's get out of here."

The droid checked the light level to make sure his apertures were set correctly, switched to record, and followed Jan into the corridor. They hadn't traveled more than a few yards when a voice called, "Hey, you! Hold it right there!" A blaster bolt served to underscore the words.

Jan shouted "Run!," fired a shot in return, and followed her own advice.

Not very speedy to begin with, A-Cee lost even more time as he paused to record Slyder, and the assortment of Imperial military personnel recruited to support him. The Captain, who was one of old man Haj's many granddaughters, had refused to take sides.

Ondi would have been proud of the way A-Cee ripped off a four-second scene and checked to make sure it was good prior to lurching away. He didn't get far, though. Slyder's energy bolt hit the center of his back, bored a hole through one of his subprocessors, and triggered an emergency shutdown. The droid collapsed as Jan looked back. She swore under her breath, ducked around a corner, and ran even faster.

Kyle burst out of the lock, ran across the deck, and spotted Rosco. He held a blaster carbine cradled in his arms and looked ready to use it.

"Has Jan arrived?"

"Not yet."

"How 'bout Waller?"

The Reb jerked his thumb up towards the cockpit. "Manning the turret."

"Okay — I'll crank her up — you cover Jan and A-Cee."

Rosco frowned. "Who died and made you Emperor?"

"Can you fly this thing?"

Rosco shook his head. "Nah, Jan's the pilot."

"Well, I can."

"Glad to hear it, Admiral, but how you gonna open those doors?"

Kyle looked at the massive pressure doors, wondered how he had missed such an obvious problem, and tried to sound confident. "You cover Jan. I'll handle the rest."

Kyle made his way up the ramp, turned towards the cockpit, and passed through the lounge. Waller dropped out of the overhead turret, saw Kyle's thumbs-up, and returned to his post.

Jan had allowed Kyle to initialize the ship's systems after the repairs were made and the access code was fresh in his mind. He entered the numbers, watched the control panel flicker to life, and grabbed a headset. "*Truly Sorry* to Hangar Control."

The woman was bored. "Control here — go."

"Request permission to depart hangar bay five minutes from now."

The controller's voice was stern. "Not funny, *Sorry*. Departure requests must be filed at least thirty standard hours prior to takeoff. Permission denied."

Kyle checked to ensure that Rosco was clear, fed power to the repulsors, and danced the ship out onto the taxiway. He hadn't flown a ship like the *Sorry* before, and she wobbled like a trooper on leave. The response came quickly.

"Control to *Sorry*! Return to your slot, power down, and lower your ramp."

Kyle tried to look in every direction at once as he spoke into the boom comm. "No can do, Control. Open the doors — or I'll open them for you."

"You don't pack enough punch," the woman countered grimly. "Return to your slot before someone gets hurt."

Kyle checked his weapon selector switches, discovered that he didn't pack enough punch, and chose a different approach instead. "Hey, Waller. See that shuttle on the far side of the bay? The one with the SoroSuub logo? Work it over."

Bolts of energy burped across the bay, hit the other ship's starboard wing, and sheared part of it off.

A klaxon sounded. Warning lights flashed. The PA system came on.

"This is an emergency. Clear the hangar deck. I repeat, clear the hangar deck. Standby for depressurization. This is . . . "

Sentients dropped their tools and ran, waddled, and, in at least one case, oozed towards the nearest lock. Kyle fought to hold the ship stationary. "Where's Jan?"

Rosco spoke into the headset he wore. "No need to panic, Admiral — she's on the way!"

Kyle saw a lock open, saw Jan start his way, and wondered about A-Cee. The Rebel agent was about halfway to the ship by the time the lock opened again and a posse spilled onto the deck. There was a Rodian in the lead, followed by Nathan Donar, and a mixed bag of Imperial military personnel. They opened fire and Rosco returned it.

Jan picked up speed, Waller fired the turret gun, and four of her pursuers fell. The rest scattered. Kyle saw Nathan duck into one of the secondary locks and felt relieved. They hadn't been friends, not in the real sense anyway, but he wished the officer no harm.

——— ⚞✦⚟ ———

Jan watched the *Truly Sorry* fade in and out of focus while it lurched up and down. Her breath came in painful gasps, her heart beat faster than it should, and lead filled her legs. She realized that the bleating noise meant something, that the air was getting thin, and she was about to die. Jan threw herself forward, stumbled, and fell. The steel felt cold beneath her cheek.

Kyle saw Jan fall, guessed the nature of the problem, and moved the ship in that direction. "Rosco? Can you help?"

Rosco, who had taken the precaution of slipping an emergency oxygen mask over his face, was already in motion. Kyle saw him, fought to slow the ship, and struggled to focus. The ramp was halfway open, which meant air was being sucked out of the *Sorry*'s cabin. Kyle fumbled for a mask, found it, and pulled oxygen into his lungs.

Rosco bent, scooped the girl into his arms, and turned. A stray piece of paper whipped past his face as the doors parted and air rushed into space. He had a minute, maybe less, to reach the ship's interior. It was that or wait for the ensuing vacuum to turn him inside out. But what about the ship? Was it there? Or had the kid left them to die?

Rosco turned, found the *Sorry* looming over him, and saw the ramp touch the deck. The Rebel took five steps, felt the ramp under his boots, and gave thanks as hydraulics lifted both of them into the ship. Not bad for a wet-behind-the-ears kid . . .

Kyle swung the speedster around, saw space suits heading for one of the ships, and wondered if he should fire on them. The *Sorry* shuddered as a concussion grenade exploded near her stern and he thought better of it.

The doors were halfway open by now. Kyle aimed for the ever-growing rectangle of blackness, applied more thrust, and ignored the controller's threats. Then, with surprising suddenness, they were free. Stars wheeled as he put the ship into a turn, and added thrust. A voice came from next to his ear. "Thanks, Kyle. It looks like I owe you all over again."

Kyle grinned as Jan dropped into the copilot's position. She was pale but determined. "You're thinking of Rosco."

Jan nodded. "Him too. How's our tail?"

"Company's coming," Waller answered laconically. "One so far."

"Let's see what kind of legs they have," Jan said grimly, and pushed the sublight drive control to max. Kyle saw a distant spark of light grow a tiny bit brighter, and felt the hull vibrate. He frowned. How much could the *Sorry* take? "What about a hyperspace jump?" Kyle inquired. "We could lose them in a hurry."

"Yes, we could," Jan agreed, her fingers moving over the controls. "If the navcomp knew our coordinates. You didn't happen to load our position, did you?"

Kyle felt blood rush to his face. "The thought never crossed my mind."

Jan turned and her expression softened. "Don't worry. The navcomp will detect whatever beacons happen to be in the area, and if that fails, run star scans till it finds a match. That'll tell us where we are."

"Which is in deep trouble," Waller added calmly. "They're gaining."

Slyder, who owned a small but heavily armed vessel of his own, had allowed the humans to provide the transportation. A logical choice considering the fact that the Governor's yacht was larger, faster, and better armed than his vessel. At least it had seemed logical, before he came aboard, found himself relegated to the status of observer, and realized how incompetent the humans were. The vast majority of the posse were officers, most of whom were giving orders, none of whom were following them. And, as if that wasn't bad enough, there was the Governor himself, constantly throwing his weight around, setting the wrong priorities.

The droid was an excellent example. Rather than leave it aboard the *Star*, and deal with it later, the Governor had brought it along. And now, when his attention should be on the speedster, Donar had focused on the droid. The machine was spread-eagled on a table while a much-abused technician sweated over it. Cables ran from a patch panel to its CPU, power supply, and subprocessor wiring harness. "I think I have it, sir — just one more connection."

The Governor, robes rustling, moved in for a closer look. Nathan did likewise. Slyder, who saw the whole exercise as a colossal waste of time, hung back.

The technician connected a cable, flipped a switch, and waited for some sort of reaction. A-Cee opened his eyes and tried to sit. Nothing happened. He remembered the chase, the programmed equivalent of pain, followed by darkness. He blinked as a trio of humans stared down at him. One of them wore a uniform.

A-Cee felt a subroutine kick in, heard the words, and knew his fate: "I am a bomb. Unauthorized access, manipulation, or interference with me or my programming, data storage modules, or other systems will result in the detonation of four point two kilos of plitex nine explosive . . . "

There was a frantic, desperate attempt to deactivate the droid and stop the countdown. But Slyder knew there wasn't enough time. All his plans, all the years of work, had turned to dust. The humans were worse than incompetent, they were irretrievably stupid, and deserved to die. Slyder drew his weapon, shot as many of them as he could, and waited for the inevitable. The trophies would go to his mother.

⊷ ⊰⬦⊱ ⊶

Kyle fought gravity as Jan put the *Sorry* into a tight turn. He was proud of the fact that his voice remained level. "What's the plan?"

"We can't outrun them," Jan said grimly, "so that leaves one choice."

"Blow our brains out?" Kyle asked lightly.

"Right idea — wrong people," Jan replied tartly.

The other vessel was closer now, so close that Kyle could see it with his naked eyes. Jan fired the *Sorry*'s laser cannons, and he watched as coherent energy stuttered towards the chase ship. It was, Kyle thought, a courageous but mostly symbolic attack, since there was no conceivable way that the speedster's relatively light weapons would overcome the larger vessel's shields. Then the yacht exploded in a ball of flames. He threw an arm in front of his eyes. "What the — ?"

The fireball died as Jan jinked to the right. The *Sorry* wove her way through a steadily expanding debris field as Kyle tried to absorb what he'd seen. "Lucky hit?"

The Rebel shook her head. "No way — nobody's that lucky. Some sort of internal explosion would be my guess."

Kyle pondered that. "What happened to A-Cee?"

Jan snapped her fingers. "Of course! They brought him around, shoved a uniform in front of his sensors, and blammo! Poor thing. I liked him."

Nathan had been wearing a class B uniform the last time Kyle saw him. Revenge, if that's what it was, brought none of the satisfaction that he had expected.

Their boots clacked against the deck as Jan and Kyle marched the length of the gleaming white corridor. Though the ship was crewed by all manner of beings, none of whom displayed the spit-and-polish exactitude expected aboard Imperial vessels, there was no doubting their enthusiasm. Crew beings hurried toward duty stations, droids whirred this way and that, and a feeling of pent-up energy permeated the air.

The recently rechristened dreadnaught *New Hope* was more than six hundred meters long. She was old, slow, and in spite of efforts to upgrade her weapons systems, poorly armed. Kyle knew all that, but couldn't help being impressed by the ship's size, the spirit of her all-volunteer crew, and the effort to make her operational again.

The dreadnaught had long been stationed over Churba as a sort of orbital war museum; the Alliance had used four deep-space tugs to break it free of the planet's gravity well and tow her away. Where they had gone, and how the refit had been carried out, were secrets. But the results were impressive. Especially from a psychological perspective, since the raid made the Alliance look strong and the Empire weak.

"So," Jan said as they rounded a corner, "what do you think?"

Kyle smiled. "You were right, Jan . . . she's impressive. Too bad a Victory-class Destroyer could fight her to a standstill."

It wasn't the wholehearted endorsement that Jan might have hoped for, so she let the subject slide. "I think you'll like Mon Mothma. Everybody does."

Kyle took note of the familiar way in which Jan used the Mothma's name, wondered if all the Rebels were so casual, and guessed that they were.

The twosome rounded a corner, walked the length of a short hallway, and stopped in front of two heavily armed guards. Jan motioned for Kyle to slide his ID card into a newly mounted scanner, waited for it to emerge, and pointed toward his blaster. Kyle felt self-conscious as one guard confiscated his side arm and the other patted him down. Apparently satisfied, the doors slid open, and Jan ushered him through. "Have a nice meeting, Kyle. I'll see you later."

The ex-officer nodded, stepped through the portal, and heard the doors close behind him. The cabin, built to pre-Imperial standards, was large but musty. Some of the furnishings were more than a hundred years old. The single occupant, a woman whom Kyle judged to be in her middle forties, turned to greet him. She had short auburn hair, greenish blue eyes, and wore a long white robe. Energy crackled around her, and Kyle could practically feel the power of her mind. She smiled and extended her hand. It was slim and cool. "Greetings, Kyle. It's a pleasure to meet you. I was sorry to hear about your father. He was an important leader."

Kyle, surprised that she knew about his father, forgot his manners. "You knew my father?"

Mon Mothma shook her head. "Not personally, but through a mutual friend, a Jedi named Rahn. He had a high level of respect for your father and sends his greetings."

Kyle was stunned. His father had known a Jedi? And earned the Jedi's respect? What else had been concealed from him?

Mon Mothma, unaware of Kyle's thoughts, gestured toward a conference table ringed with chairs. "Please, make yourself comfortable."

Kyle did as he was bid. Mon Mothma sat on one corner of the table. "Jan tells me that you want to serve as one of our agents. Why?"

Kyle, who hadn't expected any sort of challenge, was taken aback. That being the case, his words were more direct, more honest than they might otherwise have been. "I want to find the people who murdered my father and kill them."

Jan, who was watching the proceedings via an array of small, barely noticeable vid cams, lifted an eyebrow. Though understandable, a desire for revenge could cloud Kyle's judgment, and lead to mistakes. That being the case, she expected Mon Mothma to dismiss him on the spot and was surprised when she didn't.

"I understand how you feel, Kyle, believe me, we all do, but we must struggle to remain objective. The people who killed your father were evil, but the greater evil lies behind them, and sits on a stolen throne. Once we defeat that, once we defeat Palpatine, the murderers will be found. So tell me, could you put your personal needs aside long enough to tackle a mission so important, it may change the course of the Rebellion?"

Kyle felt conflicting emotions. A healthy dose of skepticism, a leavening of fear, and pride at being asked. "Yes. I think so, anyway."

Mon Mothma weighed him with her eyes. "Good. May the Maker

help me if I'm wrong, but I'm going to take a chance on you, and hope for the best. Watch the center of the table. I have a story to tell."

Mon Mothma regarded the slowly morphing holo with obvious distaste. "The Imperials call it the Death Star," the leader said grimly, "and it's an apt description given the fact that once the battle station is completed, it will be capable of destroying an entire planet."

Kyle frowned. "How?"

"It mounts the most powerful superlaser ever constructed."

Kyle tried to imagine it — a laser capable of drilling down through miles of rock, hitting the planetary core, and triggering an explosion so massive it would tear the world apart. What had Governor Donar said? " . . . The Emperor has a thing or two in store for the so-called Alliance, and your father will be revenged"? The statement made sense now — and sent a tingle down his spine. He gestured towards the holo. "Does it actually exist? Or are they planning to build it?"

Mon Mothma nodded. "Oh, it's real all right. The battle station is being constructed in orbit over the Despayre penal colony. Once completed it will measure a hundred and twenty kilometers in diameter, will have a complement of twenty-seven thousand and forty-eight officers, seven hundred seventy-six thousand, five hundred seventy-six troops, pilots, and other combat personnel, along with an additional four hundred thousand support personnel and twenty-five thousand stormtroopers.

"Besides the necessary crew, the Death Star will carry assault shuttles, blast boats, strike cruisers, drop ships, land vehicles, and more than seven thousand TIE fighters. Its hull will be protected by ten thousand turbolaser batteries, two thousand five hundred laser cannons, and more than seven hundred tractor-beam projectors."

Kyle didn't know which amazed him more, the Death Star itself, or the detailed information regarding its capabilities. "No offense, but how could you possibly know these things?"

Mon Mothma looked him in the eye. "We know because beings sacrificed their lives to find out."

Kyle nodded soberly. "And the mission?"

"The research complex where the Death Star was designed is located on Danuta. We want you to go there, find your way into the facility, and retrieve those plans. Assuming the engineers identify a weak spot, the Death Star could be destroyed."

Kyle felt his heart sink. Fighting to avenge his father was one thing — throwing his life away was another. "What you describe is little more than a suicide mission. Why not launch a commando raid instead?"

Mon Mothma nodded and touched her remote. The Death Star

exploded into a thousand points of light. A series of overlapping 3-D surveillance photos appeared. They grew successively more detailed as increasing degrees of magnification were introduced. An arrow appeared and moved from object to object. "This is the city of Trid. The spaceport is here, the fusion plant, here, and, assuming our information is correct, the research facility is here . . . Within a thousand meters of these are homes, a school, and a temple. I'd be interested in your opinion. Which is better? To send an agent? In hopes of a miracle? Or, assuming such a thing could be done, put a company of commandos on the ground, and accept the collateral damage? The Imperials would — why shouldn't we?"

Kyle felt blood rush to his face. Mon Mothma knew he'd been an Imperial officer, knew about the atrocities on Sullust, and was pushing his buttons. The knowledge made him angry. "Is this the way you get people to risk their lives? Through psychological manipulation?"

Mon Mothma nodded. "Sometimes . . . If I think it'll work."

Jan watched in open fascination as Kyle's and Mon Mothma's eyes locked and stayed that way for a long, long time. Kyle was first to look away. "Was that all? Did your agents provide anything else?"

"Just this," the rebel leader replied. "Some video of the room in which the plans are kept."

Another holo appeared over the table. This one was grainy as if shot with a low resolution lens from inches above the floor. The kind of footage a maintenance droid might capture if it had been enlisted as a spy.

Kyle watched equipment racks roll by, enough uniform clad legs to go with five or six troopers, a large expanse of highly polished floor, and there, on the far side of the room, a vaguely T-shaped construct, suspended in a U-shaped frame.

"That's it," Mon Mothma said. "The memory matrix in which the plans are kept."

Kyle was about to reply when an officer crossed in front of the lens. There was something familiar about the image. He motioned to Mon Mothma. "Would you back up, please?"

The Rebel leader complied with Kyle's request, hit play, and allowed the video to jerk forward one frame at a time.

Kyle looked and looked again. There was no doubt about it, the officer was none other than Meck Odom, his ex-roommate and best friend. It appeared that Odom's request for a Special Operations assignment had been granted. And quickly, too. Kyle felt tiny beads of sweat dot his forehead and resisted the temptation to wipe them away. "Thank you."

Mon Mothma's face was expressionless. "Do you know that officer?"

Kyle shrugged. "I thought I did — but I was wrong."

Mon Mothma nodded noncommittally and the holo disappeared. "So what's your decision? Will you take the mission?"

It was crazy, stupid, and possibly fatal, but Kyle nodded. Not for the Rebel cause, or in reaction to Mothma's blandishments, but for his father and those who died with him.

The interview ended shortly thereafter. Mon Mothma watched Kyle go, shook her head thoughtfully, and walked to the viewport. Jan entered through a concealed hatch. The leader spoke without turning. "So? What do you think?"

Jan shrugged. "He's scared — but who wouldn't be? The chances for survival are slim."

"And that bothers you?"

"Yes."

"Do the two of you have a relationship?"

"Not in the sense you mean. No."

"Could you kill him if you had to?"

Jan frowned. "Yes, if he deserved it. What are you suggesting?"

Mon Mothma turned. Their eyes met. "Katarn lied. The officer in the holo is named Meck Odom. He was Katarn's friend at the Academy — his only friend."

Jan struggled with conflicting emotions. "So? Maybe that means something and maybe it doesn't. Don't forget about the lives he spared on that asteroid, or his actions on the *Star*. Not to mention the fact that the Imperials killed his father."

Mon Mothma turned back to the viewport. "Yes, but what if the whole thing were planned? The head could be faked. What if his father is alive? Held prisoner against Kyle's actions? What if the whole thing is part of a complex plan to place a spy in our ranks? The Empire is capable of that and more. I want you to follow Katarn, watch his every move, and kill him if he flips. Can you do it?"

Jan nodded. "If I have to. But what then?"

Mon Mothma turned to take Jan's hands in hers. "The only thing better than a well-laid plan is a well-conceived backup plan. Our forces on Toprawa may have a shot at the Death Star plans as well. The problem is that while the Toprawa plans include the battle station's hull design, and life support infrastructure, the Danuta plans include additional engineering schematics, and, if we're lucky, a complete map to the offensive and defensive weapons emplacements. We need both sets to ensure success."

"You could send someone else. Someone like me."

Mon Mothma shook her head. "Katarn was one of them — he knows how they think. Besides, a man stands a better chance of getting into what may be an all-male facility."

Jan released Mon Mothma's hands. Her words took on the sound of an accusation. "And Kyle is expendable."

Mon Mothma allowed her hands to fall. The resentment in Jan's eyes was plain to see. So was her duty to the Alliance. "Yes, Jan. Kyle is expendable. We all are."

CHAPTER 6

Kyle felt lonely and depressed as he made his way through a maze of corridors, passageways, and drop shafts to the hangar deck. In spite of the fact that he'd been granted the very thing he'd hoped for, a chance to join the Alliance, there was none of the "hail fellow well met" camaraderie he'd expected. Just an impossible mission, minimum support, and a none-too-emotional parting of the ways. Yes, Mon Mothma had shaken his hand, and Jan had sent an E-mail: "Have a new mission — sorry I can't see you off — best of luck."

Pleasant enough, but not the sort of send off lavished on departing heroes. Not in holovids, anyhow. It seemed he was and would forever be an outsider. Ah well, he was on his own, which beat the heck out of taking orders. That was something he was truly tired of.

A horn beeped, Kyle stepped out of the way, and allowed the auto cart to pass. The hangar bay was just ahead and he stepped into the main lock. A group of techs continued their noisy debate as they crowded in behind him. The discussion centered around the question of which one of the ship's meals was worst — breakfast, lunch, or dinner. Kyle cast a silent vote for breakfast, smiled when dinner won, and followed the men and women out into the bay where an avalanche of stimuli assailed his eyes, ears, and nose.

Where the *Star*'s hangar deck had been only two-thirds full, this one was crammed with X-wing starfighters, assault shuttles, and a bewildering array of other craft. It was almost impossible to hear himself think over the screech of power cutters, the rattle of chain hoists, the whine of hydrospanners, and the announcements made via the overamplified PA system.

Not only that, but where Kyle had encountered just the occasional whiff of ozone aboard the liner, he now inhaled a rich amalgam of exhaust fumes, fresh paint, hot metal, bonding agents, cleaning compounds, and lubricants. The total effect was overwhelming.

Kyle spotted a sign that read "Deck Master," along with an arrow which pointed the way. The first arrow led to a second arrow, and so forth, until he arrived at the edge of a yellow-and-black striped "no park" zone. A ten-meter exoskeleton occupied the center of the space. The operator was nearly invisible within his protective cage. He yelled amplified instructions to an overhead crane operator who raised a thumb by way of reply. Their failure to communicate via comlink seemed strange, but consistent with the overall atmosphere. The decal on the front of the exoskeleton's chest plate read "Deck Master."

Kyle stepped over a power cable, ducked under a wing, and entered the striped area. A Mon Calamari, a Wookiee, and a human were in line ahead of him. Fifteen minutes had passed by the time his turn came. The DM towered above Kyle and his voice rolled like thunder. "Don't ask for a maintenance droid. They're busy right now."

Kyle shook his head. "No, sir. I'm here to select a ship."

The DM shook his head. "Can't hear you, hold on." Kyle watched with alarm as a pair of skeletal arms reached down, got a grip on his torso, and lifted him up. The DM had bushy eyebrows, bloodshot eyes, and at least three days' worth of beard. "There — that's better — say it again."

Kyle said it again. The DM raised an eyebrow. "Select a ship? What do you think this is? A supermarket? You got a chit?"

The data card was in his right-hand pants pocket. Kyle felt more than a little ridiculous as he searched for and found it. Was everyone staring at him? Or was this sort of thing so common that no one paid attention?

The DM locked his mechanical arms in place and used the flesh-and-blood versions to accept the piece of plastic. The terminal mounted on his roll cage ate the rectangle and spit it out again. Characters flickered, steadied, and scrolled down the screen. The DM read them, shook his head in disgust, and grumbled about the "metal heads on the bridge."

Kyle, who was used to an atmosphere in which superiors were never criticized, not even jokingly, must have looked concerned because the deck master chose to explain. "People in civilian clothes rarely return the ships they borrow, or if they do, we spend weeks patching the battle damage. I don't know where you folks go, or what you do out there, but it's hard on my inventory. Here — check these out, and whichever one you pick, take good care of it. The Alliance will deduct the damages from your salary."

Kyle didn't have a salary so far as he knew, but he smiled politely. The deck master laughed and put Kyle down.

Relieved to have both feet on the deck again, Kyle scanned the printout. He saw three hull numbers and the spaces they were parked in. Nineteen, twelve, and three. He left the no-park zone, found a slot number, and worked his way down a line of X-wings. Could it be? They were hot ships by all accounts, and he'd love to fly one. Assuming he could cut the mustard. Engineering students were trained to fly a wide variety of support craft but limited to thirty hours in TIE fighters. Kyle was perfectly willing to learn, however, and would like nothing better than a sleek one-seater of his own.

The numbers dwindled and Kyle's hopes went with them. A half-junked shuttle occupied twenty-two, followed by a grease spot in twenty-one, and a lifeboat in twenty. Kyle's heart sank as he inspected the pre-Empire gig that occupied slot nineteen, the courier ship that slouched in twelve, and the Corellian-built lighter that overflowed three. The *Sorry* was nowhere in sight but would have been preferable.

Kyle gave a sigh of disappointment, returned to the gig, and started a lengthy inspection of each ship's hull, drives, armament, life-support systems, and controls. It was a laborious process but necessary, since his life would depend on the choice he made.

In the end, with all the facts he could muster before him, the choice was rather simple. In spite of the fact the ship in slot three looked as if had bounced around the inside of an asteroid belt for a month or so, she was only ten years old, and Corellian-built. A good beginning for any ship. He also liked the fact that her drives had been overhauled only three months before, her shield generators tested ninety-six percent effective, and her logbooks were up to date. Last, but not least, was the fact that he related to the name painted along both sides of her atmosphere-scarred bow: the *Moldy Crow*. It sounded the way he felt — like a bird no longer accepted by its flock.

Kyle registered his choice, submitted reqs for eight hundred and seventy-eight pieces of equipment ranging from a reconditioned nav-comp to toilet paper — and received five hundred and twenty-seven of them. That left a three hundred and fifty-one item gap which he narrowed to two hundred and forty-five by "borrowing" one hundred and six tools, parts, and components from storerooms and surrounding ships, an activity that he thought went undetected but which was monitored by Jan Ors, and tolerated by the DM at her request.

And so it was that six days and seven hours after being inducted into the Alliance, Kyle Katarn set forth on what seemed like a highly improbable task. Two women watched him go. One focused on the importance of his mission. The other on him.

━━━ ⚔ ━━━

Like most of her kind, the courier ship had been built for speed, with scant attention paid to creature comforts. Jan made her way aboard, discovered that the pilot was little more than a teenager, and was amused by the pigtails she wore. The pilot accepted the agent's satchel, grumbled about women who carried too much makeup, and forced the bag into a tiny locker.

Jan considered telling her the truth, that the satchel contained energy cells for her weapons, a half dozen grenades, two knives, an ounce of plitex, a garrotte, a lock pik, electrobinoculars, a couple of comlinks, and a toothbrush, but decided to let the matter go.

The pilot turned. "You ready?"

Jan smiled. "Always."

The girl nodded. "Good. Now let's get a couple of things straight. I go by 'Jes,' not 'Jessica,' not 'dear,' and not 'honey.' This is my ship, I run it my way, and I don't need any advice from freeloading goof-offs. Got it?"

Jan kept a straight face. "Got it."

"Good. Strap in, keep your mouth shut, and hang on to your lunch. You'll be standing on Danuta before you know it."

Jan strapped into the copilot's position, thought about Kyle, and wondered how he was doing. If the pilot was even half as good as she claimed to be, and if the courier ship was even half as fast as it was supposed to be, she'd land a day before he did, and have plenty of time to reconnoiter. The hatch sealed itself, Jes brought the drives up, and the stars beckoned.

━━━ ⚔ ━━━

The run to Danuta took five days. The navcomp handled most of the piloting. When not asleep, or deeply involved in some maintenance procedure, Kyle rode an emotional roller coaster, but tried to marshal his mental forces.

There was a high as the mission began but that period was all too brief. The more he thought about the mission, the more problems he discovered, until they were like mynocks that sucked the courage from his bones.

The obvious solution was to devise a plan that dealt with the potential problems, and thereby defeat them, in his mind if nowhere else.

99

He spent a lot of time constructing clever scenarios, his hopes rising as they took shape, only to encounter a barrier so large, so insurmountable, that everything collapsed. Finally, after many hours of frustrating work, he was forced to confront the fact that he lacked sufficient information. The answers, assuming there were any, waited on Danuta. Air whispered through the *Moldy Crow*'s vents, the deck vibrated, and Kyle was alone.

Jan followed the Kubazian landlord up some twisting stairs, down a filthy hall, and into apartment 4G. The "4" was missing, but the agent had memorized the landings and emergency exits. The entire building shook as a freighter lifted off. The landlord, who had been unable to let this particular set of rooms since the last tenant, a hearing-impaired Rybet, had been murdered the year before, tried to minimize the negatives. "It gets noisy at times — but the view makes up for it."

Jan, who never turned her back on him, pulled a curtain aside. Thousands of dust motes sprang free, fell through filtered sunlight, and joined their predecessors on the floor. The window was a local product, and hadn't been washed in a long, long time. The agent thumbed the latch and pushed. Additional light poured into the room and the landlord adjusted his goggles accordingly. Exposure to the red wavelengths gave him headaches.

Jan considered the view. The airport's security fence was only twenty meters away. Beyond that, out past a line of grounded ships, the freighter engaged its in-system drives, and blasted the length of the runway. It was fast and disappeared moments later. The terminal was a low, one-story affair, and could have passed for a warehouse except for the antenna farm, and the surface-to-air missile battery that nestled against the west end of the building. There was no sign of the *Moldy Crow*.

The stench of fuel, ozone, and sewage wafted in through the window. The Kubazian wanted to slap a scent disk over the end of his trunk but thought better of it. Maybe, just maybe, the human was stupid enough to take the apartment in spite of the stench.

Jan turned toward the Kubazian, dropped some coins into his eternally ready hand, and said "Nice ambiance. I'll take it." The bag, still loaded with ordnance, bounced as it hit the heavily stained bedspread. Rebel agents had a saying: "Home is where you lay your head."

Danuta more than filled the ship's view screen and Kyle was celebrating his first planetfall when the proximity alarms went off. The reason was quickly apparent. Two Imperial TIE fighters, one to either side of his ship, appeared from nowhere. A comm transmission followed. There were no preliminaries — just demands.

"Orbital patrol vessel X-Ray-two-niner-one to unidentified freighter. Report the commanding officer's name, number of passengers aboard, cargo if any, port of origin, and business on Danuta."

The words had a sing-song quality, as if the pilot had uttered them countless times, which he probably had. Kyle felt his heart pound in his chest, reminded himself that such checks were standard, and opened his mike. The story had been rehearsed numerous times, and, thanks to the experts on the *Hope*, Kyle had the forgeries to back it up.

"*Moldy Crow* to Imperial X-Ray-two-niner-one. Roger that . . . My name's Drexel, Dan Drexel, and I'm the sole person aboard. My port of origin was Drog VI in the Corporate Sector. I've got a load of high-priority spares for the Brodsport Mining Corporation. Rel Farley's the assistant manager there . . . tell him the first beer's on me."

Farley was a Reb sympathizer, or so Kyle assumed, and was ready to confirm the agent's story. Silence ensued as the pilot checked with Brodsport, talked to his buddy on a different frequency, or picked his nose. Kyle had his credits on the last possibility when the clearance arrived.

"This is X-Ray-two-niner-one. You have clearance for Trid. Approach vectors are being uploaded to your navcomp. Stay inside them. It'll be safer that way. Have a nice day."

Kyle took note of the threat but felt a tremendous sense of relief anyway. "Roger that — *Crow* out."

The TIE fighters accelerated, curved away, and were lost to sight. Kyle allowed himself to relax a little, made contact with Trid ground control, and descended through the atmosphere. It looked as if a huge brown blanket had been thrown over the planet's surface. It was smooth at first, rounded where hills pushed from below, and wrinkled where canyons came and went.

The badlands gradually gave way to farms where hardy colonists, men and women like his father, coaxed circles of green from the hard brown earth. Sunlight winked off metal roofs, vehicles added an occasional touch of color, and a two-lane road led towards Trid.

The streets had been laid out grid-style by Brodsport engineers who saw the town for what it was — a miserable little outpost to which they were committed for no more than the duration of their contracts. The result was a community in which what few niceties there were had been tacked on later.

The spaceport was located at the eastern end of town, the direction from which Kyle was coming. It shimmered in the afternoon heat. Beyond the landing strip, and the low-lying city to which it belonged, Kyle saw a cluster of distinctly upscale buildings, and knew what they represented. The Imperial Research Facility on Danuta, the Death Star's intellectual birthplace, and, unless he was careful, the place where he would die.

He pushed the ship down, deployed the flaps, and fired retros. The *Crow* lost altitude, but way out there, on the very edge of the horizon, the agent saw an enormous black lake. It lay well within the Imperial Military Reservation, and it didn't take a geologist to see that the surface had been heated till it was liquid, and allowed to cool. Why would such a thing exist? Unless it was the result of an experiment of some kind. Kyle imagined a superlaser powerful enough to drill holes through the planetary crust and gave an involuntary shudder.

Then, with Trid ground control babbling in his ears and the navcomp beeping in sympathy, he killed forward motion, pulled the bow up, and lit the repulsors. Forces equalized and the ship hovered. Kyle checked the lay of the land, saw how the slots were configured, and danced the ship sideways.

The automated ground guide had been painted once, but that was a long time ago, and most of the covering had worn away, leaving islands of orange. Kyle followed the mottled machine to space twenty-three where he plopped down between an autohopper that wore governmental markings and a Brodsport shuttle.

The other end of the spaceport, the part that was heavily festooned with "do not enter" signs, and guarded by a squad of stormtroopers, was home to six carefully maintained TIE fighters, still gleaming from the morning wash-down. A good place to stay clear of.

Kyle ran the shutdown procedures, checked to make sure his indicators were green, and preset the emergency start-up sequence. When he left, if he left, there was a fairly good chance he'd be in a hurry. The local customs agent used a hydrospanner to hammer on the belly hatch, Kyle slipped into his Dan Drexel persona, and hurried to lower the ramp. To bribe or not to bribe — that was the question. Not that there was much doubt.

⊶ ▆◈▆ ⊷

The noise, combined with the way the building shook, brought Jan up out of an uncertain sleep. Her boots came off the sill, the front legs of her chair hit the floor, and she fought to focus her eyes. Though not especially busy by the standards of a planet like her native Alderaan, which had multiple ports a thousand times larger than Trid's, the strip was reasonably active, and she had already monitored the comings and goings of at least fifty ships, not counting TIE fighters or atmospheric craft. So she was pleasantly surprised to see the *Moldy Crow*, and, after he had secured the ship, Kyle Katarn. The electrobinoculars wobbled over the tarmac, centered on the agent, and brought him closer.

He looked tall and fit as he talked to the local customs agent, shook hands, and checked the *Crow*'s landing skids. What did she like about him anyway? Besides the fact that he'd saved her life? Was it the determined look in his eyes? The strength in his hands? Or the laugh that came so seldom she found herself working for it? She wasn't sure.

Kyle completed his inspection, sealed the belly hatch, and headed for the terminal. The action was sufficient to remind Jan of the mission she had accepted and the possibilities involved. What if Kyle was a spy? Sent to destroy all that she fought for? Her resolve hardened.

Jan checked to ensure that her weapons were loaded, set the satchel's self-defense mechanism, and let herself into the hall. The target had arrived. And she had work to do.

⚹

Having already inspected the town from the air, Kyle wasn't especially surprised by Trid's lackadaisical seediness. As with most planets, the nightclubs, strip joints, and cheap eateries sat elbow to elbow with the terminal, and the outfitters, suppliers, and parts houses were just up the street.

The local architecture could best be described as Imperial prefab with a touch of rimworld colonial. Examples could be seen in the colorful planters that hung off second-story balconies, the wrought-iron bars that protected ground-floor windows, and the trash-filled water fountain that graced the town square.

The citizens were just as basic. They fell in six categories: contract employees, who sported caps with Brodsport logos on them; hard-eyed colonists with work-thickened hands; scholarly types, whose clothes looked badly out of place; space trash like Dan Drexel, just waiting to leave; an assortment of aliens, none of whom seemed very happy; and stormtroopers who went everywhere in pairs. Partly for the sake of security, and partly so they could watch each other.

The troopers gave Kyle the most cause for concern, since he was wanted by now. They might or might not have seen his face during the last shift briefing. Their presence, and the fact that he couldn't see their eyes, reminded Kyle of the extent to which the Emperor ruled through fear. He remembered what it felt like to be that powerful, and came to the sickening realization that he had enjoyed it.

Kyle waited for a tractor-wagon combination to growl past, stepped off the curb, and crossed the square. Though careful to seem casual, Kyle had a destination in mind, and drifted in that direction. The possibility that he would look at the research facility and see a way in was more than a little remote, but he would give it a try.

As Kyle moved west, following the afternoon sun, his surroundings started to change. The buildings assumed a residential air and seemed more prosperous. Judging from the overall cleanliness, and the children who played in the street, this particular neighborhood had been set aside for research staff and their dependents. This was something Mon Mothma had neglected to mention, which might have been used in support of a commando raid.

A complex scheme that involved kidnapping a scientist and using his or her credentials to gain entry presented itself and was eliminated. Simplicity was the key, along with a healthy dose of luck.

Kyle felt something press against his back. It felt like — what? Someone watching him? But that was nonsense — wasn't it?

A seedy cafe spilled out onto a patch of carefully swept sidewalk and presented a chance to rest, have something to drink, and check his back-trail. Kyle smiled at the hostess — she looked to be no more than twelve — and followed her to a plastic-covered table. She cleared the previous occupant's dishes away and promised to return. Kyle sat, turned toward the east, and scanned the street.

— ◆ —

Jan rounded a corner, took two steps forward, and knew something was wrong. Kyle had disappeared, no, there he was, seated on the sidewalk. She pulled a wanted poster out of her pocket, pretended Kyle's face was a street map, and retraced her steps. The corner blocked his view but the question remained: Had Kyle seen her? And if he had, did he recognize her face?

— ◆ —

Kyle frowned. There had been something familiar about the distantly glimpsed figure, but he wasn't sure what. A person from town?

Probably, but he resolved to keep a sharp lookout just in case. He touched his blaster for reassurance. It was new, but not too new, and secured in a cross-draw holster. Fast, but uncomfortable when you sat. Side arms, and even heavier weapons for that matter, were common on planets like Danuta.

Kyle finished his drink, left some coins on the sticky tabletop, and resumed his reconnaissance.

The residential area was relatively small and quickly gave way to a carefully maintained security buffer, complete with pole-mounted surveillance cameras, recon droids, weapons emplacements, and a four-meter high razor-wire-topped chain-link fence. The buildings were low, sturdy affairs, at least half underground, and hardened against attack. He remembered Mon Mothma's holo and marveled at someone's bravery. Which raised an interesting question — what happened to that agent anyway? And why hadn't he or she been asked to retrieve the plans? The answer seemed obvious.

Kyle paralleled the security perimeter for a while, walking briskly as if for the exercise, and knew he wasn't dressed for it. The main gate was a massive affair, complete with a guard station, at least a dozen stormtroopers, an AT- ST, and a brace of armored ground cars. Not the sort of defenses he cared to test.

Careful lest he draw attention to himself, Kyle turned toward the east, chose what seemed like a quiet street, and followed it towards town. The reconnaissance had confirmed his worst fears. The Research Complex was essentially impregnable. The only way an unauthorized person could get in was if someone allowed them to enter.

The fact that Kyle knew someone stationed in the secured area had plagued him ever since he'd seen Meck Odom's face on Mon Mothma's holo. To force a choice between friendship and duty, to place Odom in terrible danger, went against everything Kyle believed in. After all, what could be lower than that? Yet what of the millions, the billions put at risk by the Death Star? What would they think of his moral dilemma? He knew the answer.

His feet seemed to be on automatic for the rest of the journey, as he made his way back through Trid. The *Moldy Crow*'s security system indicated that there had been no less than three attempts to enter the ship while he was gone, none of them successful. Kyle scanned the video secured by the rivet-sized lens, dismissed the would-be burglars as common thieves, and reset the system.

Once sealed, the hull was more than adequate protection against the spaceport's noise and stench. In fact, if it hadn't been for the vibration generated by the ships that used the strip, he would have been unaware of their comings and goings. His dinner, purchased from a street vendor and carried back to the ship, was delicious. Especially after five days of dehydrated food. He wolfed it down, drank a quart of local spring water, and hit the rack. Sleep came fast — as did the dreams.

He had switched places with a Rebel back on the asteroid. The hatch made a natural point of defense. There were so many stormtroopers that it was impossible to miss. Bodies were piled on bodies until they blocked the corridor. That's when the fighting stopped, medics removed their helmets, and Kyle started to scream. Every single corpse had Meck Odom's face.

⋅⋅➤⋅ ≣◆≣ ⋅◅⋅⋅

Given the fact that Kyle had spent the night aboard the *Moldy Crow*, and she had spent it within the confines of her miserable apartment, Jan assumed that he had slept better than she had. That's why she felt resentful when he opted for an early start and forced her to do likewise. She double-timed around the west end of the runway just in time to see him emerge from an eatery. Her breakfast, which consisted of a cup of tea purchased on the run, left her hungry.

Still, it was interesting to see him on the move, especially after the somewhat inconclusive meanderings carried out the day before. What was he up to anyway? Assuming that an agent with no real training — and no experience — had a plan.

Kyle stopped to get directions from a street vendor, turned down a side street, and found what he thought was the correct address. He turned, saw nothing suspicious about the woman staring into a shop window, the man emptying slops, or the droid that whirred down the sidewalk. Then, having checked once more to make sure he was in the right place, the agent climbed a short flight of stairs and disappeared within.

There was a carving over the dilapidated door and Jan strained to see what it was. It looked like a wheel, with complicated spokes radiating out from the center. Jan had the sense that she'd seen it before, but she couldn't place it.

One good thing about the situation was the fact that it allowed her to buy a sweet roll in a nearby shop. She was licking frosting off her fingers when Kyle emerged. He scanned the general vicinity, failed to see her through the plate glass window, and headed for the business district.

That left Jan in a dilemma: She could follow Kyle, and see where he went, or investigate the building and figure out why he'd gone there.

She chose the second alternative, waited till he was out of sight, and mounted the stairs. The door opened on well-oiled hinges, bells jingled, and the odor of incense filled her nostrils. The Ortolan monk had a long snout, floppy ears, and two disk-shaped eyes. His bright blue fur clashed with the saffron robe he wore. "May I be of assistance?" His voice was soft but audible over the distant chant.

A wheel of life, a monk, and the sound of chanting. Everything came together. A temple had been established in the building. There were thousands of religions within the Empire, and while Palpatine disapproved of many, most were tolerated so long as they remained apolitical. Jan smiled. "No, thank you. I chose the wrong door."

The monk bowed. "There are many doors — and many paths beyond them. Go in peace."

Jan bowed, knew she wouldn't find much peace, not for a while anyway, and returned to the street. She looked back over her shoulder. What did a temple have to do with Kyle? Or the Imperial Death Star for that matter? She could have asked, but what if the monk tipped Kyle off? He would recognize her description in a second. No, better to wait and see.

Jan took three steps and stopped. What if she'd been suckered? What if Kyle was a lot better trained than she thought he was, knew she was following him, and was determined to lose her? It seemed unlikely, but anything was possible. Especially for a double agent.

Jan broke into a run. It carried her down the street, around a corner, and onto the main drag. She stopped and looked both ways. Where had he gone? What was he doing? The answer, once she had it, was anticlimactic. Kyle, apparently at ease, was strolling toward his ship.

＊─＊─☲◈☲─＊─＊

A lot of people had filtered into the Blue Moon during the last hour or so. Spacers mostly, with a leavening of colonists, and aliens with nowhere else to go.

A mirror ran the entire length of the room, its insect-specked surface barely visible between the bottles, jugs, gourds, decanters, and squeeze bulbs racked in front of it. The club's proprietor wore a dingy apron, and polished the same section of bar over and over again, as if doing so would bring him luck.

Up toward the front, where she could be seen through the window, a dancer bumped and ground her way through a two-hour shift, her face empty of all expression, her eyes far away.

Further back, seated around a too-small table, a group of farm boys, their empties ranked before them, ogled the dancer, and bragged of exploits they'd never had.

Kyle, who occupied one of about ten booths that lined the wall opposite the bar, split his attention between the dancer and the entry-way. Not because the dancer was especially attractive, but because she was a legitimate place to look. The last thing he needed was a run-in with a "Who are you looking at?" drunk.

The afternoon and early evening had passed slowly, very slowly, and Kyle was nervous. So nervous he held the blaster cradled in his lap. Once he had made the decision to place his friend at risk, the rest had been easy. Comm calls were almost sure to be monitored, as was E-mail, which left word of mouth. The fact that Odom was a spiritualist, almost certain to visit the local temple, offered a path for communications.

Now, having set events in motion, Kyle worried lest something go wrong. What if Odom hadn't gone to the temple today? Or didn't go this week? How many days could he wait? Or even worse, what if Odom had been to the temple and came through the door now backed by a half dozen stormtroopers? People change. Odom could have. The Blue Moon had a rear exit, he'd made sure of that, but it would be covered.

The better part of an hour passed, Kyle bought round after round of nonalcoholic drinks, and refused two offers of female companionship.

Finally, at the point where he was ready to give up, Odom arrived. He wore civilian attire and looked distinctly uncomfortable.

Kyle forced himself to wait, saw nothing suspicious, and released the grip on his blaster. Odom scanned the crowd and Kyle waved. Visibly relieved, the officer nodded, said something to the hostess, and made his way toward the back. His face registered concern as he slid into the booth. "Kyle! It's you! I nearly didn't come. The security types lay traps sometimes."

Kyle nodded soberly. "You took a big chance. I'm sorry to put you at risk."

"What? And miss my chance to talk to the most infamous member of the class? No way!"

Kyle glanced around. If anyone was watching they hid it well. "Infamous? How infamous?"

"This infamous," Odom replied, pulling a piece of paper out of his pocket. "Here, take a look."

The paper was folded. Kyle opened the document, flattened it on the tabletop, and was shocked when his own face looked back at him. The Empire had used the holo from the Academy's yearbook. The crimes he stood accused of included desertion, treason, and murder. He felt vulnerable and resisted the temptation to look over his shoulder. "I didn't kill anyone. Not intentionally, anyway."

Odom grinned. "And the rest?"

"Guilty as charged."

"Which brings us to the present."

"Yes."

"I know I'll regret this question. But where do I come in?"

Kyle explained.

＊＋＝＋＝＋＋

Jan waited outside the Blue Moon, saw Odom enter, and felt sick inside. Mon Mothma was right. Kyle was about to meet with the officer he'd lied about knowing. Why? What were they up to? It was her job to find out.

Jan moved along the side of the building toward the back door. A drunk lurched out of the darkness and she shoved him out of the way. He backpedaled and fell into some poorly tended shrubbery. She ignored his pleas for assistance, turned the corner, stepped over a pool of vomit, and made her way up the back stairs. Hinges screeched as she pulled the door open and stepped inside. The rest rooms smelled of urine and the agent made a face. There was halfhearted applause as the dancer bent to collect her tips and a four-piece band started to play.

The agent spotted Odom, saw Kyle's back, and made for the adjoining booth. The hostess saw her, registered alarm, and rushed to intervene. At least two customers to a booth after 8:00 p.m., the owner was strict about that, and so was she. A half-dozen bracelets jangled as she made her way across the floor.

Jan allowed herself to be intercepted, smiled innocently, and showed five fingers. "We're a party of six. The rest will be here shortly."

Relieved, and optimistic about the evening's take, the hostess returned to her station. Jan struggled to hear. It was difficult, especially after the band swung into a rendition of "Rimmer's Delight," and the customers started to clap. She heard snatches though, including Kyle's promise to keep Odom's identity secret, and "the need to build a believable story."

The meeting ended after about thirty minutes. Odom left via the front door, and Kyle headed for the back. Jan paid for her drink, loosened her blaster, and followed. Her heart was beating like a trip-hammer. She'd killed people, more than she cared to remember, but never like this. Never someone she knew, and never in cold blood.

The door closed behind Kyle and Jan pushed it open. Drives roared as a ship lowered itself onto the tarmac a quarter klick away. She

looked around. The area appeared clear, and the ship would cover the noise she made. The possibility that Kyle might have body armor under his clothes suggested a head shot. Jan raised her weapon, adopted a two-handed stance, and took careful aim.

The old Kyle would have felt the pressure against the back of his head and dismissed it. This one drew his weapon in one smooth motion, turned, and started to squeeze the trigger. But he saw his would-be assassin's face, and stopped. Jan saw his hesitation, knew she should have fired, and cursed her weakness.

Kyle, unable to trust his own eyes, held the weapon where it was, but closed the gap between them. She'd been prepared to kill him, that much was clear, but why? The Empire, yes, but the Alliance was supposed to be above such things. Kyle knew he should shoot her, should burn a hole through her brain, but couldn't bring himself to do it.

He remembered the first time he'd seen those eyes, calm even in the face of death, centered on something he couldn't see. His arm sank and the blaster with it. Hers did likewise. Jan spoke first. "You deserve to die, Katarn. But someone else will have to do it."

The roar of repulsors stopped suddenly as the pilot shut them down. The relative silence made his words seem louder. Kyle shook his head. "You have it wrong, Jan."

"What about Odom? You told Mon Mothma you didn't know him."

Kyle shrugged. "I wanted to protect him, to leave him out of it."

"And now?"

"I pulled him in. There's no other way."

Jan allowed her blaster to slip into its holster. A pair of drunks wobbled around the corner, stumbled, and laughed hilariously as they helped each other up the stairs. She searched his face. "Why? Why would he help our cause?"

Kyle looked away and back again. "I don't know for sure. Friendship, his religious beliefs, it's hard to say."

"But you believe he will?"

"I'm willing to bet my life on it."

There was momentary silence. Jan thought about what she'd been prepared to do and shivered. If she had killed him, would it have been an act of fanaticism or patriotism? How did one tell the difference? The answer, if one existed, refused to come. She forced a smile. "Come on. Let's have dinner. Assuming we can find a restaurant dark enough to hide your face. And it's on me."

CHAPTER 7

It took three hours for Kyle to make his way across the ravine, find a path through the maze of boulders, and arrive opposite the gate marked "S-2." It was three meters tall and constructed of solid durasteel. An energy cannon might burn a hole through it, but nothing less would touch it.

Odom had explained that the gates had letter designations: E for East, W for West, N for North, and S for South. Each side of the rectangular perimeter had four or five such openings for the convenience of maintenance and security teams who would otherwise have been forced to rely on the main gate, which would be an inconvenience at least, and dangerous in case of attack.

Kyle checked his chrono, found that he had a full hour to wait, and ducked behind a rock. He was well within the range of the nearest surveillance cam and would be vulnerable until darkness cloaked his movements.

The window of opportunity, and it wouldn't last for long, would occur at precisely 2100 hours when the officer of the watch, Meck Odom in this case, would use remote testing equipment to open and close the door locks. It would be during this test, while the door was momentarily unlocked, that Kyle would slip through. That, combined with Odom's ability to momentarily override the collateral security systems, would allow Kyle to penetrate the outer perimeter. The rest would be up to him, and, assuming he made it to the extraction point, Jan Ors, who had agreed to pull him out.

Kyle remembered the night before, their mutual reluctance to kill each other, and smiled. His expression froze as stones rattled nearby.

What was it? An animal? Or something more ominous?

The agent wanted to investigate but knew better than to do so. Whatever it was might sense his movements. And what? Attack? Report his presence? Either possibility would be disastrous.

Kyle held his breath and kept a grip on his blaster. There was silence, followed by a sound similar to the first one, only closer this time. Metal rasped on metal, then moved away. Slowly, his blood pounding in his ears, Kyle started to breathe again. The machine, whatever its purpose, had left.

The sun sank over the western horizon, stars appeared in the sky, and Kyle felt very, very small. The entire mission was insane. Fear spread icy fingers through his veins. How would a more experienced agent handle a moment such as this one?

Kyle remembered the breathing exercises the Academy had taught him and put the knowledge to work. His vital signs slowed, brain activity flattened, and time stood still.

Kyle was surprised when his eyes popped open, his chrono read 2050 hours, and the moment was at hand. Widely spaced blue-green perimeter lights had come on at some point during the last half hour. They threw a ghostly glow across the rocks.

Marveling at how rested he was, Kyle turned toward the fence and did some stretches. Then, confident that his body would respond the way it was supposed to, the agent elbowed his way toward the fence. He hadn't moved more than a meter or two when a security droid appeared in the distance. It floated a meter off the ground and was mounted with no less than three auto blasters and a pair of independently controlled spotlights. They chased each other back and forth, probing the shadows for intruders, verifying the integrity of the fence.

Kyle weighed his alternatives. The lock would open in a little more than seven minutes. The droid was traveling at maybe two or three klicks an hour. There was no way to evaluate the variables precisely, so he would have to guess.

Kyle gritted his teeth, resolved to stay low, and low-crawled upwards. Loose gravel rattled away from his boots, his senses seemed unusually acute, and the droid grew larger.

The agent sprinted across the unpaved maintenance road that fronted the fence and dived into the shadow opposite the door. A quick check showed he had three minutes to go. More than he would have liked, but a necessary trade-off.

The droid moved forward, sensors scanning, searching for anything outside the parameters of what its programming classified as "normal." Was the machine faster now? Or did it only seem that way?

Whatever the truth, Kyle knew the droid would spot him before the lock opened, assuming it ever did.

Desperate now, and unable to come up with a better alternative, Kyle felt around the ground, found a baseball-sized rock, and stood straight up. He threw as hard as he could, not at the droid, but over its CPU housing, hoping to trigger a motion detector, or failing that, to generate some noise.

The rock flew straight and true, landed in the scrub, and caused a miniature landslide. The droid turned, aimed its spotlights toward the noise, and brought two auto blasters to bear.

Kyle turned toward the door, looked at his chrono, and saw the final seconds tick away. Then, just as the readout changed from fifty-nine to double zeros the agent heard an unmistakable "click." Kyle's heart was in his mouth as he gripped the T-shaped handle, gave it one turn to the right, and pushed. The door swung miraculously open and Kyle slipped through. The droid's spots washed over the door only seconds after it closed.

Kyle allowed himself a two-second celebration, checked his surroundings against the mental map created from Odom's descriptions, and started to jog. Half a klick separated the fence from the complex. A surface patrol would sweep through the area in fifteen minutes or so. That gave Kyle plenty of time to reach the entry point.

The air shaft was Odom's idea. Like similar ducts located throughout the complex, the vent was intended to collect fresh air and carry it to the sublevels below. Security was ensured by heat and motion detectors mounted inside the shafts. The only problem was that a persistent software glitch had triggered a long series of false alarms. Repair requests had been submitted, and would be acted upon, but that was a week or more away. During the interim, alarms from that particular source were routinely ignored, providing Kyle with the perfect opportunity.

The complex loomed ahead. Kyle scrambled up a bank, leaped an ornamental hedge, and arrived in front of a duracrete wall. The roof was low and readily accessible due to the fact that ninety percent of the building was underground. Kyle followed the vertical surface to a corner, found the horizontal slots intended to make the facility more interesting to look at, and climbed hand over hand.

The roof was broad and flat. There was a gravel-like substance that crunched under his boots, a cluster of antennas, a reinforced landing pad marked with four flashing lights, and yes, the top of an air duct.

Moving quietly, or as quietly as the gravel would allow, Kyle crossed to the far side of the roof. The duct was protected by a pyramid-shaped all-weather cap. His multitool made quick work of the screws — one to each side of the vent. They gleamed as they hit the roof.

That out of the way, Kyle wrapped his arms around the sheet metal, bent his knees, and lifted. There was momentary resistance followed by sudden freedom as the cover popped loose.

Kyle set the structure on the roof and peered into the pitch-black duct. He patted his belt, found the glow rod, and pulled it free. The ladder was obvious. The agent turned, stuck the light between his teeth, and lowered himself into the shaft. He found a rung with his feet, tested the metal with his weight, and started his descent.

The light wavered back and forth across bare metal as Kyle sank into the darkness. He was committed now — and it was literally do or die.

Jan had retrieved her satchel from the apartment and used most of the contents to build a tidy little bomb. She buried the device near the north side of the security fence. The explosion would take place at precisely 2145 and should be sufficient to draw at least some of the surface forces away from the main complex. Then, at 2200 hours she would pass over that exact spot in the *Moldy Crow*, hose the area down, and head for the pickup point. It was not an especially fancy plan. But it should be sufficient to the purpose.

Jan was about to enter the *Crow*'s belly when movement caught her eye. Pole-mounted lights bathed the area directly in front of the terminal. The local customs agent was there, as were half a dozen stormtroopers. The official waved a piece of paper and yelled something unintelligible. The Imperials turned, looked in Jan's direction, and started her way.

Jan ran up the ramp, hit "retract," and made for the cockpit. The battle was about to begin.

Kyle saw a large white numeral 1 and knew he had gone far enough. The ladder continued downward through a man-sized hole. Kyle stepped onto the grating provided for that purpose. The access hatch, also marked with a big white 1, stood in front of him. There would be guards on this level, lots of them. Odom had emphasized that.

Kyle drew his blaster, took a deep breath, and touched the entry plate. The door slid open, a commando appeared, and Kyle fired. The Imperial staggered, fired a shot into the ceiling, and fell. It happened so quickly there was no time to be afraid.

Kyle holstered his hand weapon, grabbed the Imperial's assault rifle, and started down the hall. The lights were relatively dim and the walls were bare. The agent knew that he had two main allies: surprise and speed. The trick was to make maximum use of both. The left-hand wall led to a door, a rather important door, one he would return to. There were other things to do first, however. An operations room appeared to the right, an Imperial moved toward the hall, and Kyle fired.

Jan bit her lip as the drives came online, quickly followed by the ship's navigation, weapons, and life-support systems. The emergency start-up sequence was fast, but not as fast as she wanted it to be.

The stormtroopers' commander saw the ramp retract, heard the drives start to wind, and ordered his men to fire. They obeyed and the *Crow*'s shields flashed as the energy bolts struck.

Repulsors flared as the lighter lifted off, and the commander gulped as the bow swung his way. To the soldier's credit he was still there, still firing his nearly useless pistol, when the belly gun cut him in half.

The commando looked surprised, tried to say something, and fell. A pair of officers turned in Kyle's direction, fumbled for their side arms, and crumpled as Kyle shot them. He mounted the platform, checked for ammo, and took what he could.

A quick glance confirmed the first door to his left, another door to his right, and a hall straight ahead. Which strategy should he pursue? Check the hall to eliminate whatever opposition might be hiding there? Or try the first door — followed by the second?

The decision was made for him when a commando appeared at the far end of the hallway and opened fire. Kyle fired in return, saw the Imperial fall, and felt blaster fire fan the side of his face. A second commando, this one backed by an officer, triggered a three-shot burst.

Kyle ducked, went to automatic, and saw the Imperials fall. Concerned that there could be more where those came from, the agent moved up the corridor, grabbed some loose power paks, and followed the hall to the left. The communications center was clear. Kyle checked, assured himself the hall was empty, and returned the way he had come.

A quick turn to the right brought him to the durasteel door with illuminated panels. Odom claimed the red key was required in order to open it, but what if his friend was wrong? Kyle approached the door, touched the access panel, and waited for something to happen. Nothing did.

Kyle was disappointed, but there was nothing to do but retrace his steps, position himself in front of the second door, and prepare for the worst. Once through, he would dash to the other side of a courtyard, open a portal, jump on a turbolift, enter the security station, and grab the key. All under fire. Not a pleasant prospect. The agent touched the control panel and the door slid open.

Jan saw the last stormtrooper fall, turned to port, and headed for the TIE fighters. If she could incapacitate some or all of the pursuit ships, the odds against a successful extraction would fall from totally impossible to very unlikely, which she saw as one heck of an improvement.

The agent fed power to the *Crow*'s repulsors which put another three meters between the hull and the tarmac. All the Imperial pilots were running for their ships by now. Easy pickings if not for the fact that one of the fighters had wobbled off the ground. The ship was pointed in the right direction. Jan could imagine the officer's frustration as he attempted to coax full power from still-cold engines and bring weapons systems online.

Jan forced herself to wait while the *Crow* stabilized, her targeting systems beeped readiness, and her cannon indicators glowed green. Both pilots fired at the same moment. The Imperial pilot's shot was too high. Jan's hit the TIE fighter head on, detonated a full load of fuel, and blew the enemy vessel apart. The entire spaceport was lit by the resulting flames.

The remaining pursuit ships were rocked by flying shrapnel, bathed in fiery fuel, and torn by Jan's cannon fire. The extraction had begun.

Two stormtroopers stood with their backs to the door. Kyle spent a fraction of a second considering whether it was ethical to shoot them from behind, then fired as one of them started to turn. He nailed the second guard as well, moved through the hatch, and felt the door close behind him.

It was dark in the courtyard. Sheer walls rose ahead of and behind him. Two sets of ghostly white armor appeared to his right. They fired and Kyle fired in return. His weapon was on automatic now, consuming energy at a prodigious rate, but equalizing the odds. The Imperials fell and blaster fire slashed from above.

Kyle turned, spotted four troopers on the walkway above, and flinched as a bolt singed his shoulder. Logic dictated that this was it, the end of his life, since no one could shoot that straight or fast . . . Unless — the thought acted like a trigger. Time slowed and his senses grew more acute. The Force was like a river that carried all before it. Those who lived in harmony with its currents were strengthened — while those who stood in opposition were tossed like chips in a flood.

Kyle stood within an eddy, chose his target, and fired. Not a long burst, but a single, perfectly aimed shot. The bolt found its mark, as did the rest.

Kyle felt pressure from the right, turned, and fired again. The stormtrooper threw his arms out as if crucified and landed on his back.

The agent exchanged his nearly empty assault weapon for one snatched from the ground and ran for one of two steel reinforced doors. It opened to his touch and his heart lurched as the Imperials swiveled in his direction. Was there no end to them?

Surprised, and apparently unaware of the battle that had been fought in the courtyard, the troopers fell while still trying to bring their weapons to bear. Kyle grabbed their reserve power paks and scanned the room. There was only one way to go — the lift.

The agent checked his weapon, touched the control panel, and aimed at the lift door. When it opened he expected to see a full squad of stormtroopers armed with everything up to and including rocket launchers. The lift opened and the platform was empty.

Relieved, but still apprehensive about what he would encounter one level up, Kyle entered and turned his back to the wall. It was a short ride but Kyle was ready when it was over. The officer, a thin man with a badly scarred face, died first, and was quickly followed by a trooper who asked for his name, and a commando armed with a doughnut.

The key lay within inches of the officer's fingertips. It pulsed with internal light and felt warm in Kyle's pocket. The trip down was mercifully uneventful as was the quick dash across the dimly lit courtyard. Lights marked the door as did the bodies sprawled in front of it. It opened smoothly and closed behind him.

A quick check of the control area on his left, and the hallway on his right, was sufficient to assure Kyle that his earlier adversaries remained undiscovered. Or were they? The impulse that caused him to look upward came at the same exact moment as the blaster bolt that blistered the paint beside him.

Kyle classified himself as an idiot for not noticing the upper-level